THE STORY OF
SCOTLAND

THE STORY OF
SCOTLAND

BY

H. W. MEIKLE

OLIVER AND BOYD

OLIVER AND BOYD LIMITED
EDINBURGH : TWEEDDALE COURT
LONDON : 39A WELBECK STREET, W.I

Sole Agents for Canada
CLARKE, IRWIN & CO. LIMITED
TORONTO

FIRST PUBLISHED IN THIS EDITION   1949
FIFTH REPRINT   1964

PRINTED AND PUBLISHED IN GREAT BRITAIN
BY OLIVER AND BOYD LTD., EDINBURGH

PREFACE

As this book has been written at my suggestion, I may be permitted to say a few words regarding its object and scope. The age (from eight to twelve) of the scholars for whose use it is intended necessarily determined the nature of its contents. For such scholars a continuous narrative of events would be wholly unsuitable, as involving a strain on their attention which is neither desirable nor profitable. If they are to derive any benefit from the reading of history, therefore, it can only be from the presentment of a succession of scenes and pictures which in themselves are of a nature to appeal to the youthful mind. And, as it happens, the history of Scotland more than most national histories lends itself to this mode of treatment.

The object of the author of the book, therefore, has been to select such persons and events as by their own intrinsic interest are fitted to attract and impress the readers whom he had in view. Necessarily it is in the legendary and romantic element in the national history that he has found his main themes for treatment. In treating such themes, however, a certain difficulty arises; in many cases the legend or romance is sufficiently remote from the actual fact of history. Is it desirable that the scholar should learn what he must one day know to be largely the product of the popular imagination and to have no existence in reality?

The legend and romance of any nation is its most characteristic mental product at a time when its genius reveals itself most spontaneously. To know the legend and romance of a nation, therefore, is to know its essential traits in a way and a degree which are not attainable from a bald narrative of historical facts. In the case of

Scotland, moreover, legend has a positive historic value. The belief in such tales as those of Scota and of the origin of the House of Stewart, firmly rooted, as it was, in the national mind till comparatively recent times, was a potent formative influence in the development of the Scottish people. It produced a sense of unity and continuity of destiny which was not the least important factor in moulding the heterogeneous elements of the population into a nation, conscious of its own individuality, and determined to preserve its integrity against all disintegrating forces.

For these reasons an acquaintance with the legend and romance of his native country is a necessary acquisition for the pupil, if he is to have an intelligent knowledge of its history as a whole. And it is in the first stage of his progress that legend is fitted to have its specific educational value. His mental outlook is that of the time when legend grew, and he is therefore prepared to benefit by whatever formative influence it may possess. And it will be generally admitted, that if, as Wordsworth says, to " nourish imagination in her growth " should be a main concern in the instruction of youth, more effectual means to that end can hardly be found than the legend and romance of their native country.

P. HUME BROWN.

University of Edinburgh.

NOTE TO 1949 EDITION

The book has been re-set, re-illustrated and re-designed so that the full benefit of modern technique in presentation may be made available to the pupil. The text is unchanged. The principles of selection given in the preface have been strengthened by time—they are probably more " up-to-date " now than when they were set down.

CONTENTS

vii

THE STORY OF SCOTLAND

THE COMING OF SCOTA

LONG, long ago, so the old, old stories tell us, there came sailing to the Green Isle, a king, a queen, and a great host of warriors. The queen was called Scota, and so dearly did the king love her that he and his fighting men called themselves " Scots."

Now many of the Scots saw that Ierne, as the Green Isle was then called, was a fair place to dwell in. So there they stayed, they and their children.

These bold Scots delighted in adventure. When they stood on the northern shores of Ierne, they saw across the waters a new land lying dim beneath the clouds. It lay towards the north of another isle called Britain.

So some of the warriors passed over the sea to that new country. There they fought many battles with the men of North Britain, and beat them. Therefore these Scots dwelt there, they and their children.

So there were at that time Scots in North Britain, and Scots in Ierne—in Scotland and in Ireland, as we call them nowadays.

THE COMING OF THE "DOVE"

Many years afterwards, a prince was born in the homeland of the Scots. When he grew up, he was so gentle and lovable that the Scots called him Columba, which means the " Dove."

Often some of his kinsmen came from North Britain to visit his father's court in the Green Isle. How eagerly Columba listened! For, though loving and gentle, the lad was high-spirited like his countrymen, and fond of wandering.

He liked also to hear of Christ, and to read His story in the beautiful hand-written books his teachers gave him. When he grew older, he wished to tell others what he had learned about Him.

One day he left the shores of Ierne, with twelve companions, to seek out his friends in North Britain. It was but a frail little boat that carried them. It had long ribs of wood covered with the skins of animals.

Yet these brave men dared the stormy waves that rolled between the two isles, and reached in safety the island of Iona. This island was opposite the shores where the Scots of North Britain dwelt.

There Columba and his twelve comrades, clothed in long white robes, took off their

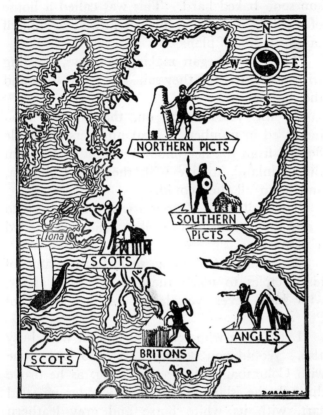

sandals and, kneeling down, thanked God for His protection.

Then they set to work to build a shelter for themselves. First of all, they made a kind of

skeleton house of branches and twigs. Afterwards
they filled in the spaces with soft mud, which the
sun soon baked hard. This was called a house
of wattles. Columba, however, dwelt by himself
in a little hut of planks.

Then they began making journeys, meeting
with many perils as they sailed between Iona and
the mainland.

As the years rolled on, the huts in Iona
increased in number. Great numbers of people
flocked from the neighbouring islands, and from
the mainland, to live with the holy Columba,
and learn all they could.

This collection of houses where men lived to
learn about God, and dwell in peace, was called
a monastery.

Afterwards Columba sent forth many of
his disciples to teach the people round about,
who had never yet heard of the Prince of
Peace.

Even those who remained behind were busy
also. Would you not have liked to have gone
with Columba, some fine morning, as he drove
through the island in his little wooden-wheeled
cart, with its white horse and grey leathern
cover? How the little children crowd around
him to get a caress from his loving hand!

First he visits his garden, for he loves all
things, birds, and beasts, and flowers.

Then off he goes to the mill, talking kindly to the driver. They pass the yellow fields of corn, soon to become bread for the monastery. And when afternoon comes, he sits in the little wooden hut with his ink-horn at hand, writing books for his scholars or copying out others. There were no printed books in those days.

Thus calmly and peacefully Columba lived his life, doing good to all around him.

HOW SAINT COLUMBA WENT TO SEE A KING

That part of North Britain where the Scots lived was called Dalriada. Now Columba knew that the land northwards and eastwards, over the mountains, was inhabited by another people called " Picts," or the " Painted People." They got this curious name, because they liked to paint their bodies to make themselves look fierce when they went to war.

They were savage heathen, and Columba longed eagerly to tell them about God. So he set off on a long and perilous journey to Inverness, where Brude, King of the Picts, lived.

There were no roads in those days. The land was covered with dark and pathless forests, where strange, wild animals roamed.

Happily Columba knew of a sea-road. Thus

he came to the southern end of the lochs that still divide the land where the Picts then lived.

Day after day he sailed northwards. At twilight he landed on the shore of the loch. Many a deer ran back startled to the woods.

As he slept at night beneath the stars, he heard the howl of the wolf, and the growl of the bear.

Yet on he held his way. In the distance he could see the torrents rushing to join the waters of the loch. How beautiful the marshes were, decked with water-lilies!

Sometimes he found little villages of wattled huts by the loch-side. How the rude villagers stared! Fierce fellows the men were, clad in the skins of wild beasts, and armed with bows and stone-tipped arrows. The women, singing as they pounded the corn between two stones, stopped to gaze at the stranger's face.

At length Columba drew near the palace of the king. It stood in the centre of the rude village, surrounded by a

ditch and a palisade.   King Brude would not
see the man of God.   He bade the gates be
shut.

Then we are told that, as Columba prayed,
the locked doors sprang open.   Tremblingly
Brude came to meet the white-robed messenger
of the King of Heaven, and to listen to his
words.   Soon King Brude and his people became Christians.

Columba had many other adventures; but at
last the angels warned him that he would have to
quit this world.   At midnight he stole into the
church, and there his disciples afterwards found
their master dying on the altar steps.   So passed
away Saint Columba.

Then other messengers came to other dwellers
in North Britain.   South of Dalriada, that is,
south of the river Clyde, St Mungo converted
the Britons.   St Cuthbert preached to the
Angles, who inhabited the land which lay south
of the river Forth.

In this way, all who then lived in our country
—Scots, Picts, Britons, and Angles—became
Christians.

THE STONE OF DESTINY

In the days of St Columba, and for many years afterwards, each of these peoples, the Scots the Picts, the Britons, and the Angles, had a separate king to rule over them. But, as both the Picts and the Scots had become Christians through St Columba, these two peoples became much friendlier.

It took a long time to bring this about; but at last Kenneth MacAlpin, King of Dalriada, became king of all the land north of the rivers Forth and Clyde. His father was a Scot, and his mother a Pict.

He would, of course, be very proud of his new title, "King of the Picts and Scots." To make it remembered he had himself crowned at Scone with great splendour.

When the crown was placed on his head, he did not sit upon a shining seat of gold. There was a throne more precious to the Scots than even a golden one.

It was a large flat stone, called the " Lia Fail," or the Stone of Destiny. You can see it to-day in Westminster Abbey, in London; and how it came to be there you will learn later.

At that time, however, it was carefully guarded in the Church of Iona; for it was said to be the very stone that Jacob used as a pillow at Bethel, when he saw the angels in his dream.

The Scots had brought it with them to the Green Isle. Those who crossed over to North Britain did not forget it, for it was held to be a lucky stone. There was an old saying about it:—

> " Wherever rests this holy stane,
> The Scots shall never cease to reign."

Thus Kenneth MacAlpin was crowned, and was king for sixteen years. When he died, he was buried in Iona.

As king followed king, each tried to be as famous as King Kenneth, and to make his kingdom larger. Yet it is so long ago since they lived, that little can be told about these kings.

But we know that a king, called Malcolm II., not only ruled over the Scots and the Picts, but also over the Britons of Strathclyde. Thus he was strong enough to fight the Angles, and to win the land between the Tweed and the Forth. This Malcolm was therefore the first " King of Scotland," and, indeed, he was the first to receive this title.

Many wonderful tales are told about the kings who reigned after Malcolm; but the most wonderful of all is the story of Duncan, Malcolm's grandson.

This Duncan was so gentle and mild that he was called " Duncan the Meek." He was greatly beloved by the people for his good deeds, but he had many enemies in those fierce, unruly times.

To fight the foe, he sent out two of his kinsmen: Macbeth, who was the son of Sinel, Thane (or Earl) of Glamis; and Banquo, Thane of Lochaber.

These two were brave men of battle, and soon the king had peace. For this reason, there were none whom the king loved to honour more than Macbeth and Banquo. Macbeth, however, was the greater favourite.

HOW THE THANE OF GLAMIS BECAME KING OF SCOTLAND

Here is the story that used to be told of Macbeth and Duncan.

It happened that Macbeth and Banquo, merry in heart, were journeying to Forres, in the North, to hold a feast of joy after their victories.

As they wended their way across the desolate moors, three old hags came to meet them.

The first cried out: " Hail, Macbeth, Thane of Glamis."

The second came and said: " Hail, Macbeth, Thane of Cawdor."

But the third declared: " Hail, Macbeth, that shalt be King of Scotland."

While Macbeth was wondering what they meant, Banquo asked them what would happen to him, and he was told that his children would reign over Scotland for many years.

Fain would Macbeth have asked many a question, but the old women vanished into air. So Macbeth knew that they were the " Weird Sisters " or " Witches."

Immediately after, there came a messenger to tell Macbeth that his father, Sinel, was dead, and that he was now Thane of Glamis in his stead.

Yet another came, saying that the king had decreed that Macbeth was to be called " Thane of Cawdor," because he had helped him in his wars.

Thus two of the sayings of the Weird Sisters had come true, and Macbeth began to wish in his heart that the third were true also.

Now the wife of Macbeth was very beautiful, but also very wicked. When she heard what the witches had said, she urged her husband to gain the crown by killing the good King Duncan.

At first Macbeth shuddered at the very thought. He remembered how generous the king had been to him. But his wife kept urging him continually to do the deed.

One day, when the soft breezes blew, and the swallows fluttered around the thane's castle, King Duncan arrived on a visit. The proud and beautiful Lady Macbeth went to meet the silver-haired old king. He gallantly gave her his hand, and so they entered the castle.

But in the dead of night, while the winds were howling and the thunder rumbling, a dark deed was done.

Two soldiers always watched the king. That night they slept, for Macbeth had given them wine mingled with drugs.

Macbeth stole in, and, taking the two dirks of the sleeping warders, pierced his king to the heart. Then, before leaving, he put the daggers, all red with blood, into the two sleepers' hands.

Now Macbeth was overcome with fear when he thought of his evil deed, but his wife bade him be merry, for now he would be king.

Early next morning, the gracious Duncan was found stiff and cold. Macbeth tried to show his sorrow by drawing his sword and killing the king's two guards, as they lay in their drunken sleep with the tell-tale dirks beside them.

But Malcolm, Duncan's son, and all his

friends saw quite well what had happened. Malcolm fled to the King of England, and Macbeth became King of Scotland.

HOW BIRNAM WOOD CAME TO DUNSINANE

When Macbeth was King of Scotland, he tried to rule justly. But he could never put the dreadful deed out of his mind. Nor could he forget what the witches had said about Banquo.

So he set two ruffians to kill him. But though they murdered him, yet his son escaped to Wales. Long afterwards, it was believed, his children, called Stewarts, ruled over Scotland.

Still, Macbeth was no happier. All men hated him. He did not rule by love, like King Duncan. He ruled by fear; he was a tyrant.

One night he went to see the Weird Sisters. He told them what he feared. " Listen," said they, " Macbeth shall never lose his crown until Birnam Wood comes to Dunsinane Hill."

Now on Dunsinane Hill was Macbeth's castle, and Birnam Wood was twelve miles from it. So the king thought himself safe. " For who," said he, " can uproot the forest and move it so great a distance? "

Yet, to make sure, he ordered all his thanes to send stones and wood to strengthen his castle.

They were also to send oxen to draw them up the hill.

A certain thane, Macduff of Fife, did as he was bid. Macbeth feared him, for he was both brave and wise.

One very warm day, the king rode out of the castle gate to see how the work was going on. As he looked, he saw a pair of oxen sink under their heavy burden.

" Whose are those poor oxen? " he asked.

" Macduff's " some one said.

" Then," said Macbeth in a great rage, " since the Thane of Fife sends such worthless cattle as these to help me, I will put his neck into the yoke, and make him drag the load himself."

When the Thane of Fife heard this, he fled by sea to England. Then Macbeth besieged his castle. He took it, and slew its brave defender, Lady Macduff, her sons, and all her servants.

Macduff arrived safely in England. There he found Prince Malcolm, the son of the murdered Duncan, at the king's court.

He told him all that had happened, and tried to persuade him to go back to Scotland and take the crown from Macbeth.

Malcolm at first refused. "I am very wicked," he said; " I should be even a worse tyrant than Macbeth."

" Well," said Macduff, " but you can become better."

" That may be; but I never keep my word."

At this Macduff burst into tears, saying that he would never see his beloved land again.

But Malcolm had only said this to see what kind of man the Thane of Fife was. So he bade him be of good cheer. Together they went to the King of England, who gave them many soldiers. They set off, and soon drew near Dunsinane Hill. Macbeth was within his castle, for he was now so afraid that he never stirred outside its walls.

It happened that one day there came a messenger to him with a strange story. The man declared that, as he watched upon the hill, lo, Birnam Wood began to move!

"Liar!" cried Macbeth, "if thou speak'st false, upon the next tree shalt thou hang alive. But if thy words be true, I care not if thou dost as much for me."

Yet the messenger had said what seemed to be true, for Malcolm had ordered every man in his army to cut down boughs, as they marched through Birnam Wood. These they carried in front of them, so that no one could tell the number of soldiers.

Though Macbeth called to mind the words of the Weird Sisters, yet he fought bravely. At last he and Macduff crossed swords. Quickly the Thane of Fife laid low the murderer of his wife and children. He cut off Macbeth's head, and carried it to his prince.

Soon afterwards Malcolm was crowned King of Scots at Scone.

HOW A PRINCESS OF ENGLAND
BECAME A SAINT OF SCOTLAND

King Malcolm was known as Malcolm
" Canmore," or " Big Head "; but he was
" Big-Hearted " as well, and soon his people
loved him dearly.

When he had ruled over Scotland for ten
years, a great event took place.

One day there might have been seen a ship,
with torn sails, creeping up the Firth of Forth.
Slowly it made its way, for it had braved many
a gale.

At last the anchor was cast in a little bay, not
far from the king's palace at Dunfermline. The
people all along the beach had been watching the
ship, and they sent word to the palace.

The king's messengers came to see this
strange vessel. Never had they seen such a
large ship, or such finely dressed lords and ladies
as were therein. When they heard their pitiful
story, they made them welcome.

Their tale was soon told. They had fled from
England, for a great warrior, called William
the Conqueror, had crossed from France to
England, killed the king, and made himself
ruler.

So Prince Edgar who should have been,
king, set out with his mother, Agatha, and his

two sisters, Margaret and Christina, and many high-born Englishmen, to seek help from the King of Scots.

Malcolm was delighted to welcome them. They were really old friends whom he had often met at the court of the King of England, when Macbeth ruled Scotland.

There was soon much merrymaking to cheer the exiles' hearts. It was then that Malcolm fell in love with the Princess Margaret.

A royal wedding soon took place. The king had added the brightest jewel to his crown; for did not Margaret mean " Pearl? "

Malcolm's lady was as good as she was beautiful. When she rose early in the morning, she used to go and pray in the little chapel the king had built for her.

Then she would wash the feet of twelve poor people. She wished to show that, though she was a great lady, yet she was tender and loving.

Twenty-four little children, who had neither father nor mother, always lived in the king's palace. The queen liked to teach them and speak kindly to them.

Sometimes she used to walk in the woods with the king. Then they would sit down beside a little stream. There Queen Margaret read to the king; and, though he himself could not read, yet he often bent to kiss the books his lady prized so highly.

If he thought she liked one better than the others, he sent it away secretly to get it made more beautiful. What a pleasant surprise for the queen when she saw it again with a golden cover, glistening with gems!

Often Queen Margaret used to sit beside her ladies as they sat making dresses for the poor, or robes for the priests of the chapel.

When people saw all this, they said, " She is better than a queen. She is a holy woman." So they called her " Saint Margaret."

HOW THE QUEEN LIVED IN
DUNFERMLINE

It is a bright summer morning, and the sun lights up the king's palace at Dunfermline. Suddenly the doors swing open, and a gay throng of lords and ladies ride forth.

Here is the gallant King Malcolm with his gracious queen. What fine clothes they wear! Margaret likes to see all around her beautiful, and the king does everything he can to please her. Every year, the queen sends her merchants to distant lands to bring back the finest cloths.

Tall, stalwart lads and fair maidens ride behind. These are the princes Edward, Edmund, Edgar, Alexander, and David, and the princesses Edith and Mary. Many of their attendants are English friends of the queen. Malcolm has given them lands in Scotland, and now they are always in his company.

Others are Scots like Malcolm himself, and speak Gaelic. I think we might have seen a frown on some of their faces that fair morning, for they do not like the king's new ways. They think that the old ways of Macbeth were better. Yet they say nothing, for they fear Malcolm's anger.

Sometimes Margaret rides out without the king. Perhaps she spies a beggar by the roadside. All the lords and ladies stop, while the queen gives away her cloak to the poor man. It may be a tartan one, a new kind of cloth the queen has just had made.

At other times she quits the roads, and turns into a large field near the palace. There she sits, while the poor and needy come and tell her their troubles. Then she relates them to the king, and so helps him to be just and kind.

If we entered the palace with her, what a change we should see! The old bare walls are covered with tapestries sewn with pretty pictures. Cups and dishes of gold are on the king's table, and many noble lords and ladies are his servants.

The king has also another palace at Edinburgh, on the Castle Rock. Many a time the eager rowers bend their backs, as they take Malcolm and his wife from the Hope to the Queen's Ferry, on their way to Edinburgh.

Now William the Conqueror was very angry when he heard how Malcolm had welcomed Margaret and her friends. Many battles took place, but at last the two kings lived at peace.

William's son, however, quarrelled with the King of Scots.

Malcolm was so angry that he gathered a great army. Queen Margaret, who was ill, did not wish him to go, but he left her safe in his strong castle at Edinburgh.

With his sons Edward and Edgar, he marched from Edinburgh through the district called Lothian, till he came to the Cheviot Hills. Then he crossed into Northumbria, as that part of England was called.

Now Queen Margaret became weaker. One day she said, "Perhaps a great calamity is happening this day to Scotland." It was too true. Her husband and Prince Edward were slain in battle that very day.

As she lay dying, her son Edgar arrived with the sad news. His mother only glanced at his face. "I know it," she said; "I know it, my boy. Tell me all the truth." Then, as she prayed, she peacefully passed away.

She was buried in Dunfermline, in the church she loved so well. Twenty years later, Malcolm's body was brought from England, and laid beside his wife's.

HOW PRINCE DAVID BECAME EARL
OF HUNTINGDON

When King Malcolm died, his three sons, Edgar, Alexander, and David, one after the other, ruled over Scotland.

Even the people of England heard of their noble mother. For during the reign of Alexander, his sister, Edith, was married to Henry, King of England. She was known as Queen Matilda.

Evening meal in the great hall of a noble lord

David accompanied his sister into England. There he married a lady, who was also called Matilda, and who was very wealthy. When David married her, he became Earl of Huntingdon, in England. The Prince of Scotland was an English earl.

In those days all the land was supposed to belong to the king. So David went to London to claim his land.

One day the King of England sat in his royal hall, surrounded by all his nobles. Outside, on horseback, was the Earl of Huntingdon, in shining armour.

On his head was a helmet. Over his body was a shirt of mail. His legs and his arms were covered with armour. In his steel-gloved hand he carried a spear. A sword hung at his belt. Even his

horse was protected with armour. He was an
iron man on an iron horse.   Beside him is a

mailed " knight," not
quite so richly armed.
A knight's son acts as
a " squire " or page.
He helps the great earl
from his horse.   Then
the page unfastens his
lord's helmet.

The earl enters the
hall. His spurs are off,
his sword is gone. He
approaches the king,
kneels down, places his
hands in the king's,
and swears to obey
him.

This is how he pays
" homage " to the king,
and becomes his "man"
or " vassal."

When the earl ar-
rived home at his castle
at Huntingdon, the
same thing was done.
He divided his lands among his knights, who
became his vassals.   They gave it to the
" yeomen," and they became the knights' vassals.

The king did not ask the earl to pay rent for his lands. Instead, he made him promise always to be ready for war.

When the king wanted to gather an army, he sent to his earls for the fighting men. They sent for the knights, who gathered the yeomen. Soon the king had a great host.

Of course, David only promised to obey the king as Earl of Huntingdon. He was his own master as Prince of Scotland.

When Alexander died, David became King of Scotland. He gave estates or lands to many of his English friends, who became his vassals. Most of them also were already vassals of the King of England.

A merry life these lords lived in their strong castles. These were often perched on a steep hill beside a rushing stream. To make them stronger, they were surrounded by a moat, or ditch, and a great wall.

The noble lord passes his time in hunting or fighting. When evening comes, the great tables are placed down the centre of the hall. The upper one, raised a little above the rush-covered floor, is for the lord, his lady, and their sons and daughters. It is laden with wheaten bread, wine, and venison.

Lower down are the yeomen. Lowest of all are slaves. Oat-bannocks and ale are on their tables.

When the feast is over, the earl makes a sign to the minstrel, whose golden locks fall in clusters over his crimson robe. In his hand he carries the harp he can play so well. As his fingers move joyfully over the strings, he tells a story. Perhaps he sings how a gallant knight in glittering armour saved his helpless lady-love.

WHY KING DAVID BUILT
HOLYROOD ABBEY

" It befell that one day," says an old story-teller, " King David came to visit his castle at Edinburgh. There was much forest in the land. Close to Edinburgh was the forest of the King's Park.

" There were many wild beasts in it in those days: deer, foxes, and wild boars.

" Now the day was a holy day, when in those far-off times people went to church.

" But the gallant nobles urged the king to go a-hunting. The priest said, ' No, it is a holy day.' Yet so eagerly did the king's young courtiers desire to chase the deer, that he yielded.

"All entered the forest. Loud bayed the dogs, and soon the deer ran from their hiding-places. The wood was filled with the music of the chase.

" The king, near Salisbury Crags, under the shadow of a leafy tree, awaited the coming of the deer. Suddenly a deer with great speed made for the king. His horse, frightened, rushed off. The stag struck horse and king to the ground, and wounded the king's thigh with his horns.

" Now, by chance," says this tale-teller, " the king tried to save himself by catching hold of the deer's horns. In doing so, he knocked a rood, or holy cross, against them. At once the stag fled away, and vanished among the leaves.

" The wounded king was carried in a litter to the castle. That night he heard a voice saying, ' David, build a monastery where the stag pierced you.' The king did so, and called it ' Holyrood Abbey.' "

Thus runs this pretty tale of bygone times. We know that King David built many other monasteries and abbeys besides Holyrood. There, as in the days of St. Columba, men lived a calm life in those unruly days.

The king gave much land to the monks who lived in these monasteries. Indeed, he gave away so much, that a king who ruled after David called him " a sair saint."

Yet the monks were often very clever and busy men. They healed the sick; they read and wrote books; they painted pictures; they built churches. These churches were of carved stone, not of wood, as in the days of St. Columba.

They taught the children of the nobles. They were good gardeners also; and the king often gave them poor land, which they soon made rich and fertile.

Sometimes King David gave away lands to the merchants. They paid him money that they might live together and trade. They soon had a little town built, with a wall round it for protection.

Let us enter the gate. What queer narrow streets! We can hardly see the sky, for the houses seem to meet overhead.

Here are the carpenter and the smith at work in the open air. There the apprentice, with shrill voice, tells the worth of his master's wares.

There are no fine shop windows, but the goods are piled up on great stone slabs in front of the stalls.

The town cross stands in the centre of the little square. Here the king's laws are read out to the people, for few can read for themselves. Here the townsfolk come together from time to time to discuss their affairs. Here the king's steward comes to gather his lord's rents.

But 'tis sunset, and the curfew rings out from the church steeple near at hand.

"Curfew" means, "Cover, or put out the fire." For all the houses are of wood, and might easily be destroyed, if the fires were left to burn all night.

All retire to rest, and nothing is heard but the heavy tread of some townsman. He tramps along the lonely street, in the moonlight, with steel cap on head, and pike in hand, to watch the walls and gates of his good town.

THE STORY OF A FIGHT IN EARNEST

David for many years was very friendly with the King of England who had married his sister. Their daughter was called Matilda, and her father made all his lords promise to crown her queen when he died.

In those days, the fierce lords and barons did not like to obey a queen. When King Henry died, they did not keep their promise. King David crossed the Borders to fight, like a gallant knight, for his helpless niece.

His army made a brave show as it marched along. There were the fierce men of Galloway, from the South, covered with skins of wild animals. There were David's mail-clad lords and knights, on their prancing steeds, with lance and fluttering pennon.

Behind them came the sturdy yeomen, in iron cap and leathern coat, armed with battle-axe and spear. Archers from Teviotdale were there, and fighting men of Lothian.

This great host met the English at Northallerton, in the north of England. Before the battle took place, an aged English baron, called Robert the Bruce, came to King David. As an old friend of the King of Scots, he begged the king to make peace.

Tears streamed down David's cheeks, and he was just about to yield. At that very moment, however, the leader of the men of Galloway cried, " Bruce, thou art a false traitor." Bruce, in anger, left the Scottish camp.

When an aged bishop, with tears in his eyes, called on all men to fight for their homes, the English swore to conquer or to die.

The fight began. The English fought round their standard. It was a great mast of a ship, with four flags streaming from it. On the top was a casket with bread taken from the altar.

In the battle, the men of Galloway, having no armour, began to give way. But Prince Henry, David's son, with his knights, rushed on the English and scattered them " like spiders' webs."

After the fight had raged for a long time, an English soldier cried, " Here is the head of the King of Scots." And there, sure enough, was a head on his spear.

The Scots, believing that their king was slain, lost heart and began to give way. In vain did David, who was not even wounded, show himself to his men. The Battle of the Standard, as it was called, was lost. David had to make peace.

He ruled for fifteen years after this. His successor was William the Lion. He got his name because he put a lion on his armour as his sign.

D

When a warrior went into battle in those days, he was so covered with armour, that nothing could be seen but his eyes, peering through holes in his helmet.

Therefore, each knight had a mark—an animal, or a sword, or a bird—painted in bright colours on his shield, to show who he was.

THE STORY OF A FIGHT IN MAKE-BELIEVE

William was as brave as a lion, and liked war, whether in earnest or in make-believe. The knights of those times were so fond of fighting, that they often played at it like a game.

This game took place on a large level bit of ground. It was carefully barricaded. A great stand was built for the lords and ladies. A Queen of Love and Beauty was chosen to give the prize. Then the knights fought each other in make-believe, though many were often killed in these " tournaments," as they were called.

Each knight burned to win honour in the fight. Perhaps the lady he loved best was watching to see if the scarf she had fastened to his lance was still streaming above the fight. At the end of the day, the best knight was crowned with a crown of leaves.

Now once William the Lion led his army into England, as far south as the town of Alnwick. There he and his knights held a tournament under the walls of the town.

By chance, a mist came down, and hid the king from his army. When the mist cleared away, William and his knights found four hundred horsemen riding against them.

The king at first thought they were some of his own soldiers. When he saw they were English he did not hesitate for an instant. " Now," he cried, " we shall see which of us are good knights."

But the brave king, who was trying to fight four hundred with sixty, was taken prisoner. The English rode off with their prize before the Scottish army, although near at hand, knew what had happened.

With his legs tied beneath his horse's body, King William was taken before Henry II., King of England. This ungenerous king would not set him free until he had done homage, not, like King David, for his estates in England, but for the whole of Scotland.

To save their king, the Scots agreed to this shameful bargain. For fifteen years Scotland had to obey the King of England.

At the end of that time, Henry died. His son, Richard the Lion-hearted, who succeeded him, was as brave as William the Lion. He wanted to go to fight the Saracens, heathen warriors who had conquered Palestine. They would not let Christians visit the Holy Land.

But Palestine was far away. Richard needed a great deal of money to take his army to battle in that distant land.

So he made a new bargain with King William, who was still in prison. He said: " Pay me ten thousand merks, and I will set you free. And, if you promise not to make war on England when I am in Palestine, I will not ask you to be my vassal, except for your estates in England. I promise that Scotland shall be free again."

William joyfully agreed, and returned to Scotland. The two countries became friendly, and for a hundred years the two nations lived in peace.

" The English," says an old story-teller, " could roam without harm through Scotland as they pleased, on foot or on horseback, this side of the Cheviot Hills, and beyond them. The Scots could do so all through England, though laden with gold."

HOW A KING TAMED THE " RAVENS "

For four hundred years the islands in the
north and west of Scotland, and even the mainland in the north, did not belong to the King of
Scots.

These parts of the country were ruled by the
Danes, or Norsemen. These Danes were also
called " Vikings," or " Creek-men," for they
came sailing from the " creeks," or little bays of
Denmark and Norway.

These Norsemen were bold sea-rovers. They roamed about the Northern Seas, with no home but the waves.

Their long, narrow boats were called " keels." These had often as many as twenty-four oars. The prows were usually beautifully carved with dragons' heads, and each boat had a single mast with a great broad sail. At the top these pirates flew a blood-red flag with a dusky raven upon it.

The vikings were therefore called the " Ravens." These " fierce heathen of the Northern Sea " sailed in companies, with a petty king as their leader.

After creeping along their own coasts, they would dare the open sea in many a storm, till they came to the shores of England or Scotland.

There they sailed up the creeks wherever there was a town or abbey. Then, landing, these sea-rovers took the people by surprise. The young were carried off as slaves; the old were slain. The booty was piled on board, and before the country-folk could come together, the pirates were off.

In the days of Kenneth MacAlpin, King of the Picts and Scots, a viking vowed he would neither cut nor comb his fair hair till he had won the Orkney and the Shetland Islands. He kept his vow, and his countrymen dwelt there ever after.

As years went on, they got farther south. They landed on Iona, and killed the monks. Then they burned the church, and took away its cups of silver and gold, and the priests' robes covered with jewels. In all the churches prayers were said for help against these heathen robbers.

They continued to plague Scotland till the time of David I. Alexander II. died in Argyll, while on his way to give them battle. But Alexander III. tamed the ravens, and this is how it happened.

In his day, the lord of the vikings was Hakon, King of Norway. He was also ruler of the Orkneys, the Shetlands, and the Hebrides. Alexander sent to him, offering to buy the Hebrides. He refused to sell them. A quarrel broke out, and next year, in July 1263, King Hakon set sail with one hundred and sixty keels, and many thousand men.

He sailed round Scotland till he came to the Firth of Clyde. King Alexander was ready for him. But first he sent monks to King Hakon to beg for peace. The king treated them kindly. A great deal of time was spent going backwards and forwards between the two kings.

This delay pleased the King of Scots, for he was only pretending. He knew that about this time of the year fierce gales blew. Just when King Hakon began to think he was being tricked, the storm came on.

For two days it raged. Even the Norse King's stout ship of oak, with its great gilded dragon, was almost dashed to pieces on the rocks at Largs. Many others were driven ashore.

The country-folk rushed down to kill the foe they had feared so long. When the Norsemen landed, the Scottish knights fell upon them, and almost drove them into the sea.

At last the Danes fled by night to their ships. They sailed away round the Mull of Cantyre. But it is said that Hakon, to save time, sat in his great ship while his men drew it across the narrow neck of land at the north end of Cantyre.

He reached Kirkwall, in the Orkney Islands only to die of shame at his defeat.

Alexander III. gained the Hebrides, and added them to his kingdom; but the Orkney and the Shetland Isles still belonged to the King of Norway.

"WHEN ALEXANDER OUR KING WAS DEAD"

Now that the Danes no longer plagued the land, the king journeyed all over the country to see that men obeyed the laws. He was now called the " Peaceable King."

One night he set off from Edinburgh to visit his queen at Kinghorn. He came to the Queen's Ferry.

" Do not cross, my lord the king," said the ferryman; " the night is dark, and storm-clouds fly across the sky." But the king passed over in safety.

The storm of wind, and rain, and snow broke as he landed on the other side. Yet with two guides he set out along the narrow bridle-path by the seashore. His horse stumbled in the dark. The king was thrown over the cliffs, and killed. You can see the place to this day.

All Scotland was in sorrow for their " King of Peace." This is what they said:—

> " When Alexander our king was dead,
> That Scotland ruled in love and le,[1]
> Away was wealth of ale and bread,
> Of wine and wax, of game and glee.
> Then cry to God, for only He
> Can save us in perplexity."

[1] law.

The Scots were in great trouble. Alexander's sons were all dead. His daughter, Margaret, who had married the King of Norway, was also dead. Her little daughter, Margaret, called the "Maid of Norway," was living at her father's court. She was only four years old when her grandfather died.

At that time the King of England was called Edward I. He was one of the cleverest of the kings of England. When he heard what had happened, he sent to the six nobles who had been appointed to rule Scotland, and said: "Let my son, Edward, marry the Maid. Then, when I am dead, they two will rule both England and Scotland."

The people of Scotland agreed. They thought it was a wise plan. There would never again be war between the two countries. But they made Edward promise that Scotland would always be a free country, and that its king would never be the vassal of England's king.

So when all this had been settled, the King of England got ready a ship to bring home the Maid. It was filled with robes and jewels. But they did not forget "raisins and figs and ginger-bread," for the little girl. However, she sailed in one of her father's ships. She reached the Orkneys safely, but there she became very ill, and died.

Who was now to rule Scotland? Thirteen nobles came forward, each wanting the crown. Who was to decide? At that very time, King Edward, seeing how things stood, asked the Scottish nobles to meet him at Norham Castle, on the Tweed. They did so.

Now the King of England really wished to make Scotland a part of England. So he said, very cunningly, "You must all become my vassals in Scotland as well as in England." He wanted to forget all about the generous deed of Richard the Lion-hearted.

What could the nobles do in their perplexity? Many of them were already vassals of King Edward, because of their lands in England. They agreed to the bargain. Then Edward decided which of them was to be king.

There were really only two who had any right, John Balliol and Robert the Bruce. Balliol was the grandson of the eldest daughter of David, a brother of William the Lion. Bruce was the son of the second daughter.

"The eldest son always succeeds his father. The eldest daughter is before the second. Balliol is king." So said King Edward. Balliol was crowned at Scone. But he had to do homage to the King of England, just as William the Lion had done to King Henry.

Then Edward went home, well pleased to

think that Scotland was now just a part of England.

THE STORY OF " TOOM TABARD "

Balliol's reign lasted from 1292 to 1296. But the people of Scotland did not like him. They laughed at him, and called him " Toom Tabard," " Empty Gown." Though he wore a king's fine robes, he was never a real king.

The King of England knew the kind of man he was, and treated him like an ordinary noble. Once, for example, a wine merchant complained to Edward that Alexander III. had not paid him for some wine. Balliol had to go to London, and defend himself like a common thief.

At last, even Balliol's spirit was roused. When King Edward ordered him, as his vassal, to leave Scotland, and help him to fight the King of France, he refused. Instead, he made friends with Edward's enemy.

From the days of Balliol, Scotland and France were always willing to help each other against England.

Edward, in his wrath, led a great army of his English vassals towards Scotland. He reached Newcastle, and again ordered Balliol to obey him. Balliol once more refused. " The fool! " said Edward, " since he will not come to us, we will go to him."

He crossed the Border, and besieged Berwick. The town was not difficult to take. Its walls were low. On one side was the sea, where the King of England had his fleet. But the people of Berwick were quite sure of being able to defeat Edward. They used to mount the walls and cry names at the English soldiers. They called the king " Longshanks," on account of his long, thin legs.

This made Edward very angry. He ordered his ships to attack the town. But they were caught on the sandbanks, and the Scots burned them.

Then he attacked it by land. The Scots fought bravely, but the town was taken. Young and old, women and children, were put to the sword.

Again Edward bade Balliol come and submit, and again he refused. The Scots were defeated at Dunbar. Then Edward marched through the kingdom, no one daring to meet him.

Most of the Scottish nobles had estates in England, and they were afraid they might lose them, if they fought against the king.

Everywhere the nobles promised to obey him ever after. Among others, Robert the Bruce, and his son, did so. So, at last, Balliol submitted to Edward.

He came to the churchyard of Stracathro,

near Brechin, where Edward had sent a bishop to meet him, for Edward would not come himself.

No crown was on Balliol's head, no sceptre in his hand, no royal robes he wore. Clothed in white, carrying a wand, he confessed that he had been in the wrong. Edward sent him south to England. He ended his days in France.

In all the castles of the Scottish kingdom, Edward placed his own soldiers. Everywhere the Scots went, to church or to market, there were their hated and cruel foes.

Then Edward returned home a second time. He carried off the Stone of Destiny, and placed it in Westminster Abbey, where it is to this day.

As he looked at it there, he thought of the old saying. " This time," said he to himself, " the Scots are surely mine."

HOW A LAD WENT A-FISHING, AND WHAT CAME OF IT

When Edward returned to England, he left behind him several of his nobles to rule Scotland. One of them was called Hugh Cressingham. He tried to get as much money as possible from the Scots for his royal master. Therefore the Scots hated this governor who treated them so cruelly.

They would have liked to fight for their
freedom against the English, but they had no
leader.

At last they found one they could trust and
obey. His name was William Wallace.

Many years after this hero's death, a minstrel
called Blind Harry sang
of his deeds. Afterwards,
he wrote them in a book.
He tells us how Wallace
tried to save his country.

William Wallace was
not a noble. His father
was a simple knight,
who lived near Paisley.

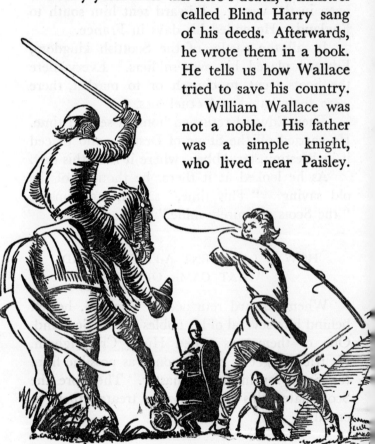

Here William grew up, a fearless youth, with a fair face, light brown hair, a bold eye, and a strong arm.

Blind Harry tells us that one day, Wallace, when a lad, went a-fishing near Ayr. A boy was with him to help him to carry the rods, and the fish he hoped to catch.

After a good day's sport, they set out for home. On their way, they met five English soldiers riding to Glasgow fair.

" Well," said one of them, " let me see if you are a good fisher."

" Why! " cried another, on seeing the fish, " you must give them to us."

" Oh! " said Wallace, " you may have half of them."

" Nay! " exclaimed the Southron, " but you must give us all for our master."

" Never will I do that," answered Wallace boldly.

" You dare say that to an Englishman," said the soldier, drawing his sword.

Wallace had not even a dagger, but with his fishing-rod he struck the man, with right good will. The sword fell from the soldier's grasp. Wallace seized it at once, and laid him low. Two others he slew, and the rest fled.

When the English governor heard of this, he sent other soldiers to capture Wallace. So he had to flee to the hills, and remain there in hiding till the deed had been forgotten.

When he was grown up, Wallace had another adventure with the English. At this time he was staying in Lanark.

One Sunday, on the way to church, he saw a very beautiful young lady. He fell in love with her at once, and soon afterwards married her.

One day, dressed in green, with a jewelled dagger by his side, he was strolling through the town. Some English soldiers passed him.

"Why has a Scot such a fine dagger?" cried one.

"Methinks you jest with me," said Wallace.

"Does a Scot dare to reply to an English soldier?" said another. Blows were struck. Other soldiers came to their comrades' help. Wallace, fighting bravely, was driven down the street.

When he saw he was at his own door, he knocked. His wife opened it, and Wallace rushed in. Quickly the door was shut again, and Wallace escaped to the hills, by a door at the back of the house.

THE FIGHT AT STIRLING BRIDGE

When Haselrig, the English governor of Lanark, heard what had happened, he sent soldiers to take Wallace. They burned his house, and Wallace's wife perished in the flames.

"Now," says Blind Harry, "a true woman who had served them long went and told Wallace of the cruel deed." Great was his grief. His companions wept also. For his friends too had fled from the town to help Wallace against the hated Southron.

At last their leader said, "Cease, men, this is but sorrow in vain. We cannot bring her to life again. Let us live to avenge her death."

As soon as darkness fell, Wallace with thirty companions crept into the town. Haselrig was sleeping in his great house, but he was awakened by a loud knock at the door.

"Who makes this noise?" he cried.

"Wallace, whom you have been seeking all day," was the bold reply. "Now you must pay for your cruel deed."

With that he drew his great sword, that no one else could wield, and killed the governor with one stroke.

Soon there was a great uproar in the house. The townsfolk joined Wallace and his men.

Before next day dawned, not an English soldier was to be found in Lanark.

Many bold men now gathered to fight under Wallace's banner. The common people were glad they had at last found a man to lead them against the English foe.

There were not many great lords in his company. They were all very proud, and many of them were afraid that they would lose their estates in England.

" Who is this Wallace," said they, " that we should obey him ? " So this brave man had to try to free Scotland without their help. So successful was he, that the English were driven out of many of the castles.

The English began to see that they would lose Scotland, if they did not make a great effort. While Wallace was trying to take Dundee, an English army was sent to help the town.

When Wallace heard this, he marched south to meet the enemy. He reached Stirling, where he awaited the coming of the English.

The leader of the Scots had few men. Nor had they been trained to fight. But each man had been cruelly treated by the English, and burned with love for his country.

Wallace was a skilful general. He placed his army on the slopes of the Abbey Craig, a hill near Stirling, with the river Forth flowing at the foot.

There was then but one narrow bridge across the Forth. Only two men could ride abreast across it.

When the Earl of Surrey, the English general, drew near, he sent monks to ask Wallace to make peace.

" Go back and tell your masters that we are not here to ask for peace. We are fighting to free our land for ever from the kings of England. Let them come when they will. We defy them to their very beards."

Now there was a Scot, a traitor, in the English camp. He told Surrey that he knew of a way across the river where the water was shallow.

But Cressingham cried, " Let us not waste time; let the fight begin! "

The Scots, perched on the opposite hills, saw the English begin to cross the bridge, two by two, with the Three Leopards of their banner gleaming in front.

Not a Scot moved till, at midday, half the English had crossed. Then Wallace's spearmen rushed down upon the foe.

So fiercely did the Scots fight, that the Southrons began to try to recross the bridge. In the confusion, horse and foot, knights and

men, were driven into the river. Hundreds were drowned.

The other half of the English host, on the other side of the river, fled. Their leader, Surrey, never drew rein till he found himself safe in Berwick. Cressingham was slain. The Scots divided his skin among them. These were fierce times, and he had been hated for his cruelty.

Many flocked to join the victorious banner of the leader of the Scots. Food was scarce, as the English had burned all the corn in the fields. So Wallace marched into Northumberland. There, for three months, the Scots lived in the midst of plenty. They burned and slew, even as the English had done in Scotland.

Wallace now became Sir William Wallace, and was called the " Guardian of the Kingdom of Scotland. "

HOW THE HERO OF SCOTLAND DIED

While his generals were being defeated in Scotland, King Edward was carrying on war in France. When he heard of Wallace's victories, his anger was terrible.

He made peace with France. With a great army of soldiers hardened in war, he marched across the Scottish Border. His ships crept along the coast to keep him company. From this fleet he got food for his soldiers.

But, though he reached Kirkliston, between Edinburgh and Linlithgow, no Scottish army came to meet him. Wallace was as wise as he was brave. He slowly retreated, burning the corn in the fields as he went.

The army of the King of England, far from the fleet, began to be in want. The soldiers began to quarrel. This was Wallace's chance to take them by surprise.

At that very moment, two Scottish nobles, it is said, brought word to King Edward that Wallace and his army were near Falkirk.

Edward set out to meet " the rebel " as he called him. He marched to Linlithgow, and encamped there. During the night, his horse trampled on him, and broke two of his ribs. Next day, however, he mounted his great war-horse, and set out, bold as ever, for the battle.

He found the Scots ready to fight. They were divided into groups. In the centre of each group were spearmen on horseback. Round about them, in a ring, were other spearmen on foot. They had their pikes pointed outwards to the foe. Each body of men was like a wall of spears. On the side of these groups were a few Scottish nobles.

" I have brought you to the fight, let me see how you can dance," said Wallace.

The English knights rode against the Scots at full gallop. Bravely the spearmen stood their ground, but the Scottish nobles fled. Many an English lord fell never to rise again, for the coats of mail they wore were very heavy.

King Edward now brought up his archers and slingers. Each archer had twelve arrows, and used to boast that he carried twelve men's lives at his belt. Every arrow killed a man.

The Scots could not stand against this fearful shower. They retreated in good order to a wood behind them, and Edward gained the day. This was in 1298, about a year after the battle of Stirling Bridge.

Once more Wallace had to live among the hills in dens and caves. For seven long years the English hunted for him. During this time all the Scottish nobles again promised to obey King Edward of England.

But Wallace would never do so. At last, Edward said he would give a great sum of money for his enemy's head. One Scot was ready to betray the hero for gold.

One night, Sir John Monteith was at supper with his friends. In the centre of the table was a loaf. Suddenly a servant came in, and turned the loaf upside down.

Immediately Sir John knew that Wallace was sleeping in a cave near at hand, and that this servant had stolen his great sword and dagger as he slept.

Wallace was easily captured by the soldiers that very night. He was taken to London, and tried by King Edward's judges.

"Wallace, you are a traitor," said one of them.

"I never could be a traitor," answered that brave man, "for I never was a vassal of the King of England."

But he was put to death as a traitor. His head was placed on London Bridge. His body was divided into four parts, and hung on gibbets at Newcastle-on-Tyne, Berwick, Stirling, and Perth.

As King Edward rode across London Bridge, and saw the head of Wallace, he must have said to himself: "Scotland's hero is dead. Scotland is mine at last."

HOW ANOTHER LEADER CAME
TO SCOTLAND

Though Wallace had been so cruelly put to death, yet the Scots never forgot his brave deeds. They were ready to fight again, whenever another hero came to lead them.

But now they had no hope. The English again ruled the land. The soldiers of King Edward were in every town and castle.

Yet, six months after Wallace's death, the Scots had another leader. His name was Robert the Bruce, Earl of Carrick. His grandfather was that Robert the Bruce who had wished to gain the crown when the Maid of Norway died.

Bruce had been brought up at the English court. He had estates in England as well as in Scotland. He was an Englishman as much as a Scot.

No one in all England was a braver knight. In the tournaments, his pennon was always on the winning side.

During the days of Sir William Wallace, as we have seen, he had sometimes fought for him and sometimes for King Edward. But when Wallace was dead, it came into the heart of Bruce to try to save his country.

So he made a bargain with John Comyn, a

nephew of Balliol, who had once been king. This John Comyn was also called the " Red Comyn." He had great estates, and was a powerful noble.

" Help me to gain the crown of Scotland," said Bruce, " and I will give you my lands. Or give me your lands, and I will help you to become king."

So these two lords agreed to help each other. But the Red Comyn was a traitor. He told King Edward about the bargain.

King Edward, as you know, was very cunning. He treated Bruce kindly. All the time he had made up his mind to put him to death. But one day, by mistake, he let fall some words at dinner showing what he meant to do.

One of Bruce's friends heard these words. He sent secretly to the noble a pair of spurs and twelve silver pennies. Bruce guessed what this strange letter meant. " Haste away from danger," said the spurs. " Flee at once; we will help you on your journey," said the silver pennies.

Snow lay on the ground as Bruce and his companions stole out of the great town at twilight. They rode northwards. It is said they shod their horses the wrong way to put their pursuers off their track.

At last they arrived at Dumfries, in the south of Scotland. Here Bruce met the Red Comyn. The two nobles met as friends. Then they went into the church, near at hand, to talk. Bruce's companions remained outside.

Bruce and the Red Comyn walked up and down inside the church. Their voices grew louder. They were quarrelling. Bruce was telling Comyn that he knew he was false.

In a moment of anger, Bruce drew his dagger and, even on the altar steps, plunged it into his enemy's breast.

Then he rushed out of the church, trembling at his awful deed. His companions looked at him in surprise.

"I doubt," said he, "I have slain the Comyn."

"You doubt!" cried Kirkpatrick, one of his friends, "I'll mak' siccar." He ran into the church and killed the wounded man.

HOW A FAIR LADY CROWNED
BRUCE

Now that the Bruce had done such a wicked deed, he knew that King Edward would never forgive him. The friends of Comyn longed for vengeance.

Bruce saw that he must be bold. With a

few friends he set out for Scone, to be crowned. On the way, he met the knight who was to help him to free his country—Lord James Douglas.

A blithe young man he was at all times. Men liked him for his sweet and gentle ways. He knelt on the ground, and swore to be faithful and true to Robert the Bruce.

When the little company arrived at Scone, they found the Bishop of Glasgow there. He was a true Scot. Now he brought forth the royal standard with its gleaming lion, which he had hidden away in Scotland's dark days.

It was not a scene of grandeur. The Stone of Destiny lay in Westminster Abbey. Edward had carried off the crown and the royal robes. Only five earls, four bishops, and an abbot dared to come to the crowning of the king.

Robert the Bruce sat upon the bishop's seat, and a brave lady, the Countess of Buchan, placed a gold band on his head. Thus the Bruce became Robert, King of Scots.

The anger of the King of England was kindled against the Scots and their king. Old though he now was, Edward gathered a great army to punish them.

But before setting out, he assembled all the great nobles of his court. Then he took a vow that he would never rest till he was really king of Scotland. When he had done this, he would go to Palestine and fight, like Richard the Lion-hearted, against the Saracens.

As he was ill, he sent on this great host in front of him. It reached Perth. The Scots sent word to the English leader, the Earl of Pembroke, that they would fight that day. But the English said that they were too tired, and promised to meet them on the morrow.

It was a delightful midsummer's evening, and Bruce and his men prepared to spend the night in the woods of Methven. Suddenly the English came upon them. They had broken their word.

Never did Bruce fight more boldly. Three horses he rode were killed. "I have the king," cried an English knight as Bruce's horse again fell. But a Scot rushed forward with another steed, and the king escaped.

Many of Bruce's friends were taken and put to death. The new-crowned king had to live, as Wallace had done, among the hills and glens of Scotland, hunted like the deer.

But he was not alone. Beside him were his queen and her ladies to cheer him. For these brave dames dared to suffer for their country, and bear many hardships.

Lord James Douglas was there too, as blithe as a lad. He was the hunter of the party. He set many a cunning snare for hares and rabbits, and knew how to fish the burns for trout.

Merry was their life in the woods, though they were often closely pursued by the English. Douglas cheered them with his jests and pranks.

Winter was now approaching, and the queen and her ladies would not be able to endure the rough life of the hills. So it was agreed to send Nigel, the king's brother, to accompany them to Kildrummy Castle, in Aberdeenshire. Many a year was to pass before the king saw his queen again.

HOW THE KING WENT TO SEE
HIS BIRTHPLACE

When the queen had left for Kildrummy Castle, Bruce and his two hundred men struck deeper into the mountains. They came to Loch Lomond, and wished to cross.

There was but one little boat, half-filled with water, which Douglas found. They baled it, and all afternoon it crossed and recrossed the loch, carrying two men and a rower each time.

At last they all safely landed on the other side, some by the boat, some by swimming, their clothes in bundles on their heads. The king helped to while away the time as they waited, by telling them stories of brave men in ancient times.

Between Loch Lomond and the coast there were great forests in those days. Here they spent many months hunting and fishing.

But even here they were not safe from the English; so they sailed to Rathlin, a little island near the north coast of Ireland. There, while the English ships of war searched all around, Bruce lived among the simple fisher-folk.

Dreadful news came from Scotland. The English had taken Kildrummy Castle and put Nigel, the king's brother, to death. The queen had been sent a prisoner to the Tower of London.

The Countess of Buchan, who had crowned the king, was shut up in Berwick Castle. A cage made of lattice, strengthened with iron, was placed in one of the dungeons. In this the brave Countess had to live for many a dreary year.

How Bruce mourned for his brother! How he bewailed the cruelties done to his wife and her ladies! As he lay in his miserable hut in the island, he began to think that he would never succeed in freeing Scotland. He made up his mind to go and fight the Saracens.

Just at that moment, it is said, he happened to notice a spider swinging to and fro from the roof. It was trying to stretch its thread from one beam to the other. Six times it swung, and six times it failed.

F

" Now," said the king to himself, " I have been six times defeated by the English. If the spider succeeds the seventh time, I will take fresh heart and try again."

The spider tried again. How keenly Bruce watched it as it swung! It succeeded. " Then," said the Bruce, " I'll try again too."

Lord James Douglas was also beginning to lose heart. He begged the king to let him cross to the Island of Arran, and see if he could do anything for his country's cause.

The English held Brodick Castle in this island, but they felt so safe that they were careless. Douglas with a small force came upon them suddenly, and took great stores of armour and provisions. Then he sent for the king.

With three - and - thirty small ships Bruce crossed over to Arran. When he landed, an old woman led him and his men to a woody glen. The king blew his horn. " That is the Bruce," said Douglas gaily. Soon the band of heroes were together again.

Now as the king looked over the water, he could see dimly the coast of Ayrshire. There lay Turnberry Castle, the place where he was born. Alas, it was also in the hands of the English.

He made up his mind to try to capture it. A spy was sent to see if any brave Scots yet remembered their lord the king. If so, the messenger was to light a beacon on Turnberry Head at a certain hour.

Cuthbert, the spy, landed at dark near the castle. He found the English everywhere, and did not dare to give the signal.

Anxiously Bruce watched on the chosen night for the glare of the beacon. Yes, there it was, a great red glow in the distance! Off they set in the boats to strike a blow in freedom's cause.

As they came ashore, Cuthbert was there to tell his story. " I lit no fire, my lord the king. Indeed, I hastened to the shore to warn you as soon as I saw the blaze someone else had made."

Some were for going back. But Edward Bruce said, " Never again will I cross the sea. Here I stay for better or for worse."

Not a sound was heard as the brave three hundred crept noiselessly to the hamlet near the castle. For all wore rough shoes of deerskin. Then they raised a great shout, " A Bruce! a Bruce! " and rushed on the sleeping foe.

The hamlet was taken. Lord Percy, who held the castle, fearing to venture out, kept its gates shut. Laden with spoil, Bruce retreated to the hills of Galloway, in the south. He had tried the seventh time, and had begun to succeed.

THE STORY OF THE DOUGLAS
LARDER

" The Good Sir James," as Douglas was now called, was ever ready for bold deeds. About this time he thought he would like to go and see his castle in Lanarkshire.

He took but two companions. They were dressed as country folk, for the English held the castle and the land. At night they came to the house of Thomas Dickson. Now this Thomas was a true and faithful yeoman, and glad was he to see his lord.

He told Sir James that many would like to fight again under the old banner. So, by night, he visited these friends, and told them their lord was near at hand. They made a plan to take the castle. This is what happened.

Palm Sunday was near, a day when all went to church to make it beautiful with green branches. When that day came, all the English soldiers set off for St Bride's Chapel about a mile from the castle.

The country people had gathered at the church door. Many of them carried their flails in their hands. All entered the church.

Suddenly there was a great shout of, " A Douglas! a Douglas! " Away went the flails, and out flashed the swords hidden beneath their coats.

The English were completely surprised. They were either killed or made prisoners. Then Douglas and his friends set off for the castle. The great gates were open. The porter and his wife were cooking a great dinner!

The Scots sat down to a right good feast. Then they collected all the arms and food they wished to take away. Next they made a great pile of all that was in the castle, barrels of wheat, and meal, and malt. Over it they poured the wine and ale.

Then they killed the prisoners, and flung their bodies on the top. Last of all, they set fire to the great heap. The castle was burnt to the ground. No English could ever take shelter in it again. This grim deed was known as the Douglas Larder.

Again Douglas took to the hills. He liked, he said, to hear the lark sing better than the mouse squeak. He liked the green fields and the hills better than a gloomy castle.

So Douglas returned to the king, full of the good news. At this time the king was in great danger; for in Galloway, where he now was, he had many enemies.

One was called John of Lorn, a friend of the murdered Comyn. He had almost surrounded the king, and hoped to take him prisoner.

By some means or other, he had a blood-hound that had once been the king's. John of Lorn and his men set out to hunt Bruce to death, taking the hound to track him.

Off it went, tugging at the long belt that held it, eager to be near its old master. In vain did Bruce try to puzzle it. He divided his band of followers into three little groups, then into six. But it was all to no purpose.

At last, none remained with the king except his foster-brother. Five men of Lorn were close behind them. These the king and his companion slew.

Again they heard the baying of the blood-hound. What was to be done? Luckily a brook was close at hand. So they waded down-stream.

When the dog came to the place where they had entered the water, it sniffed and sniffed. But it could not smell the trace of its master in running water. John of Lorn was baffled once more.

THE STORY OF A DAY'S
ADVENTURES

Tired and weary, Bruce and his companion journeyed on through the forest. There they met three armed men. One carried a sheep on his shoulders.

" Where are you going? " said the king.

" To join the king," said they.

" I can lead you to the place where he is," said the Bruce.

As the king watched the three men, he saw them look at one another. They suspected who it was that spoke.

When the Bruce saw this, he told the men to walk on in front till they knew each other better. In this way, they came to a lonely hut, where they put up for the night.

Even here the king was on his guard. He kindled his own fire. He and his foster-brother agreed to watch by turns through the night. But, tired with their day's adventures, they both fell asleep.

In the dead of night, as the fire burnt low, the three traitors rose. Noiselessly, with drawn swords, they crept near the sleepers, and raised their weapons to strike. The king awoke. Jumping up, he drew his blade. At the same time he kicked his foster-brother with his foot to warn him, but before he could rise, the traitors killed him.

It was now one against three. Bravely the king swung his good sword. Soon the three lay dead at his feet.

Sad at heart, for he had loved his foster-brother dearly, he continued his way. He came to a farm-house. Cold and hungry, weary and worn, the king dared to knock. He cared not whether friend or foe were inside.

" Come in," said a woman's voice. He entered. " Who are you? " " I am a traveller, and have lost my way." " All travellers are welcome for the sake of one," said the dame. " Who may that one be? " asked the Bruce. " It is our sovereign lord the king," she answered. " Though he is hunted like the deer, I hope yet to see him rule the land."

" Since you wish him well, good dame," said the king, " know that I am King Robert the Bruce."

You can picture this true woman's delight. " But where are your men? " she asked.

The king told her how he had been chased by the hound, and how he had lost his men. " Nay," said she, " but I have three sons who will be true to you till death."

She brought them to the king. They knelt and vowed to be ever loyal and faithful men.

After a homely meal, King Robert wished to see if his new followers could shoot well. He called the eldest, and told him to aim at two ravens perched on a rock some distance away. He pierced both with the same arrow.

The next son shot a raven as it flew overhead. It fell dead at his feet. The youngest missed.

Years afterwards, when the king came to his own again, he wished to reward the old dame for her help.

"Jist gie me the wee bit hassock o' land atween Palnure and Penkiln," said she. The king did this, and each son got his share. The emblem or crest of the eldest son, when he became a knight, was two ravens with an arrow through both heads.

As Bruce was about to retire to sleep, a great noise of horses was heard outside. Quickly the three sons sprang to defend their lord.

But it was the Good Sir James with one hundred and fifty horsemen. That night they attacked two hundred English, as they slept in the open, and defeated them.

This was the beginning of success. More and more men flocked to join their king. When Bruce met the English in open fight at Loudon Hill, in Ayrshire, he was left master of the field.

HOW THREE CASTLES WERE
WON FOR THE KING

During all this time, King Edward had been waiting to hear of the capture of his enemy. At last he grew so impatient that he set out for Scotland once again. He reached Burgh-on-Sands, on the English side of the Solway, only to die.

He had made his son, Edward, promise to carry his bones before the English army, and never to rest till he had crushed Scotland for ever.

But when he died, his son led his army back to London. There, in Westminster Abbey, they buried Edward I. On his tomb was written, " Here lies Edward I., the Hammer of the Scots."

But the army of the King of Scots grew bigger every day. One day Douglas brought Randolph to his uncle, the king. He had to join the English to save his life. Now he wished to show that he was a true Scot.

One dark night, he and thirty companions started to climb the steep rock on which Edinburgh Castle stands. Their guide was a young soldier, who had often by night escaped this way from the castle to see the lady he intended to marry.

Noiselessly, like cats, they made their way in the dark.   They rested half-way on their perilous climb.

In the stillness of the night they heard a voice crying, " I see you." Some stones rattled down the rocks, but not a man moved as he lay close to the rocks.

Luckily it was a false alarm.   It was only an English soldier trying to play a trick on his comrades.

Randolph and his men arrived at the top, and scaled the wall with rope-ladders. The castle was taken.

Soon the king's banner floated over another stronghold. A farmer, called Binnie, used to take hay to the English soldiers in the Castle of Linlithgow. Like a good Scot, he tried to capture it for his king.

One dark night, some of his friends crept up towards the castle, and hid themselves near the gateway. Early next morning, Binnie, as usual, set out for the castle. Under the hay on the cart were eight armed men.

Leisurely they made their way to the castle, the farmer walking by the side of his horse. They passed the outer door, but there was also an inner door, called a " portcullis."

The portcullis moved up and down on pulleys, like a window. The bottom was covered with spikes to crush everything underneath, if let down suddenly in the hour of danger.

When Binnie's cart was underneath the portcullis, he drew his sword and cut the traces. The men sprang out of the cart. The soldiers ran to let down the portcullis, but the heavy cart was in the way.

The friends of Binnie rushed out of their hiding-places. The castle was taken, and its walls thrown down, to save it from falling again into the hands of the English.

Nor was the Good Sir James idle. He hit upon a good plan for winning the Castle of Roxburgh.

This castle was surrounded by fields. If the Scots had boldly marched against it, they would have been seen a long way off.

But at dusk Douglas ordered his men to throw long dark cloaks over their bright armour. Then, by twos and threes, they crept on their hands and knees towards the castle.

It was a fine summer's night, and one of the ladies of the castle was enjoying the coolness of

the evening breeze. As she gazed across the ripening fields, she saw some dark specks in the distance. She told the watchman. " Oh," said he, " it is just some cattle creeping home."

So the lady sat down to nurse her child. As she hushed it to sleep she sang:

> " Hush ye, hush ye, little pet ye,
> Hush ye, hush ye, do not fret ye,
> The Black Douglas shall not get ye."

The name of Douglas had become a terrible one. The English used to tell their children, when they were naughty, that the Douglas would carry them off.

So still the lady sang:

> " The Black Douglas shall not get ye."

" I am not so sure of that," said a gruff voice behind her. At the same time a steel-gloved hand was laid on her arm. It was the hand of the Black Douglas himself.

The Scots had climbed the castle rock. The alarm was given, but in vain. Once more another castle was won for the king.

"HOW FELL THE FIERCE
DE BOUNE"

One after another, the English were driven from the castles. King Robert took great care always to level them to the ground, so that his enemies might not capture them again.

At last only Stirling Castle flew the banner of England. Edward Bruce, the king's brother, surrounded it, so that neither food nor men could be sent in.

But the King of England never even tried to help the garrison. For Edward II. was not a mighty warrior like Edward I. He liked to hold great tournaments at his court, but he did not care for battle in earnest. He loved pleasure better than gaining a kingdom.

So the English governor made a bargain with Edward Bruce. He promised to give up the castle to the Scots, if Edward II. did not come to help him before Midsummer Day of the following year.

King Robert was not pleased. He liked to take the English by surprise. Now he would have to fight a great battle in the open.

Edward II. at last determined to do something for his brave garrison. Even Edward I. had never led such a mighty host

to hammer the Scots, as now marched against
the Bruce.

The Scottish camp was in the Royal Park, near
Stirling. Alas, Bruce had not even half as many
men as the English king, and only five hundred
mail-clad knights! But who of King Edward's
army could equal Douglas, or Randolph, or
Edward Bruce?

Bravest and wisest of all was the king. He
drew up his army very skilfully. On one side of
the Scots flowed the Bannock Burn. Between
them and this brook were two bogs. A little
to the right was harder ground, covered with
trees.

Here the king ordered holes to be dug " as
deep as a man's knee." These were covered
lightly with turf. Great iron spikes were placed
here and there to lame the horses of the knights
when they charged. Then all those who did not
fight, the servants and the camp-followers, were
sent to a hill behind.

The English first tried to steal into Stirling
on the left, where Randolph held command.

" See," said the king to him, " a rose has
fallen from your chaplet." He meant that his
nephew might have won glory if he had been on
the watch.

Off Randolph rushed to drive the English
back. But the enemy had twice as many men,

and the Scots seemed lost in such a host of foes. Douglas begged the king to let him go to the help of his comrade.

" Nay," said the king, " Randolph must save himself. I will not break my ranks."

At length he consented, but as Douglas approached, he saw that Randolph did not need his aid.

" Halt! " cried the gallant Sir James, " let us not take from Randolph the glory of the fight." The king's nephew had won back the rose for his chaplet.

Meanwhile, the king rode along the ranks putting the Scots in battle array. Though he was covered with armour, his men knew their king by a golden band round his helmet. As his great war-horse was resting for the fight on the morrow, the king rode a little palfrey.

The story is that, when an English knight, Sir Henry de Boune, saw the king so poorly mounted, he thought he could easily unhorse him, and so win great glory for himself.

Spurring his charger, he dashed furiously with levelled spear against the King of Scots. Bruce's men held their breath for fear.

As the lance almost touched the king, he turned aside.

" High in the stirrups stood the king,
  And gave his battle-axe the swing.
  Right on De Boune, the whiles he passed,
  Fell that stern dint—the first—the last!—
  Such strength upon the blow was put,
  The helmet crashed like hazel-nut;
  The axe-shaft, with its brazen clasp,
  Was shivered to the gauntlet grasp!
  First of that fatal field, how soon,
  How sudden, fell the fierce De Boune! "

The Scottish nobles chided the king for thus risking his precious life. " I have broken my good battle-axe," was all he said.

" BRUCE'S ADDRESS TO HIS ARMY "

Scots, wha hae wi' Wallace bled!
Scots, wham Bruce has aften led!
   Welcome to your gory bed,
    Or to victorie!
Now's the day, and now's the hour;
See the front o' battle lour;
See approach proud Edward's power—
Chains and slaverie!

Wha will be a traitor knave?
Wha can fill a coward's grave?
Wha sae base as be a slave?
   Let him turn and flee!
Wha for Scotland's king and law
Freedom's sword will strongly draw,
Freeman stand or freeman fa'?
   Let him on wi' me!

By oppression's woes and pains!
By your sons in servile chains!
We will drain our dearest veins,
   But they *shall* be free!
Lay the proud usurpers low!
Tyrants fall in every foe!
Liberty's in every blow!
   Let us do or die!

THE BATTLE OF BANNOCKBURN
24th June 1314

" Now," says an English story-teller, " the English in the fore-part of the Sunday night, drunk with wine, feasted with great din. The Scots kept their watch in praying and silence, burning with the love of their country and freedom."

Early in the morning the Scots were seen to kneel. A bare-footed monk, carrying a crucifix, passed before each Scot, blessing him.

" Look! " cried King Edward, " these men kneel. They are begging for mercy."

" Yes," said an English knight, " but not from you. They ask it from God. These men will either win the day or die upon the field."

" So be it," said the King. " Sound the charge."

The English horsemen rode at full speed against the Scots. The shock as they met, might have been heard miles away. But the Scots stood firm as a rock.

Many of the English fell into the bogs. Others were caught in the pits that Bruce had so cunningly prepared for them.

Meanwhile, the arrows of the famous English archers fell like rain upon the Scots. But Bruce was ready for them also. He sent among them at full gallop a body of horsemen. As the archers had only their bows and arrows, they were soon scattered.

So the battle fiercely raged. Nothing was heard but the clash of steel, and the groans of the wounded and dying. Many an English knight, in heavy armour, fell, never to rise again.

The English began to give way. At that very moment, they thought they saw another army coming to help the Scots.

These were the servants and camp-followers coming over the hill. It was ever afterward called the Gillies', or Servants', Hill.

With blankets tied to tent poles for flags, and any weapons they could lay their hands on, they were rushing down the hill to get their share of the plunder. The English thought that it was another army coming to the help of the Scots.

They wavered—their ranks broke—they fled. The burn was so choked with dead bodies that men passed over it dry-shod. King Edward

fled to Stirling Castle. "Stay not here," said the governor; "no one is safe."

With three hundred men he rode for his life to Dunbar. Close at his heels rode the Good Sir James. Woe betide the unlucky Southron who fell out by the way! The king reached Dunbar Castle, and escaped by a fishing-boat to England.

He left seven hundred knights dead upon the field. Great numbers were taken prisoners. They got their freedom by paying large sums of money. It is said that "Scotland became rich in a single day."

All the English stores fell into the hands of the King of Scots. Edward had brought from England many rich dresses for himself and his knights. There were also richly embroidered robes for his priests. They were to be worn when they held a service in some great church, to thank God for victory.

Casks of wine were also found, as well as large machines for slinging stones. For as yet there was no gunpowder or cannon.

Edward had even brought a poet with him to write a poem about the battle he had been so sure of winning. The poet was taken prisoner, and Bruce would only let him go free when he had written a song telling of the victory of the Scots.

Best of all, the king was able to get back his brave wife and daughter, and their ladies. For eight weary years they had lain in English prisons.

The Battle of Bannockburn set Scotland free for ever from the English. Never will Scotland forget her two heroes, William Wallace and Robert the Bruce.

THE LAST DAYS OF THE HERO-KING

For fourteen years after Bannockburn the Scots continued to wage war. Many an army, led by the Black Douglas, or the brave Randolph, returned across the Border laden with booty.

At last, in 1328, the Scots and the English made peace. This agreement was called the Treaty of Northampton.

It was arranged that the war should finish. Scotland was for ever to be free. To make the two countries better friends, Prince David, King Robert's son, married Joanna, daughter of Edward of England.

Meanwhile the King of Scots tried to rule wisely the kingdom he had won. He called a great meeting of his earls and barons. Nor did he forget the townsfolk who had helped him in the wars. Each town sent chosen men to sit in the " Parliament," as this meeting was called.

This Parliament made many good laws. It also gave the king the right to gather money from his people. With the money he rebuilt many of the castles he had destroyed during the war.

One of these castles he built at Tarbet, on Loch Fyne, in the country of his old enemy, John of Lorn, who was now dead.

The king made several journeys to see that it was strongly built. Once when he was not there, the mason built the walls twice as thick as he had bargained for. The king rewarded this man for doing his work so well.

Here came Douglas and his friends to fight their battles over again, as they sat feasting in the hall. In an old book we read that the king spent 2s. 2d. for birchen boughs to strew on the floors of their rooms.

And the king would ever have his jester, Patrick, at his side. He wore a many-coloured dress with a pointed cap of jingling bells. His duty was to tell jokes to cheer the heart of the king and his guests.

At last, King Robert, worn out with the many hardships of war, went to spend his last days at Cardross, on the Clyde.

Here he built himself a palace. It was

thought to be a fine building in those days. Were not its windows even of glass!—a rare thing in Scotland.

A beautiful garden surrounded the palace, and many a happy day the old warrior-king spent quietly among the flowers.

Sometimes he went yachting on the river; for he loved the water, and had built many a gallant vessel to sail the seas.

" Hawking " was another of the king's sports. In hawking he used falcons. These were a kind of hawk. When the king went a-hunting, his falconer rode by his side with the falcon perched on his gloved hand. A hood covered its eyes.

If the king saw a bird, he bade the falconer take off the hood. Up flew the falcon till it was right overhead above the bird. Then quick as lightning it dropped on its prey, and killed it. When the falconer blew his whistle, it returned to its perch.

So, happily and peacefully, the days passed away. But at length King Robert grew feebler, " so that there was no way for him but death."

So he called his nobles and bade them honour and serve his little son David. Then, as they stood weeping around his deathbed, he spoke thus to the Good Sir James.

" Sir James, my trusty friend, you know that I have had to fight hard for my kingdom.

When I was in great danger, I vowed to God to go and fight the foe in the Holy Land. But, though I know now my body cannot go thither, yet will I send my heart to fulfil my vow. And, because I know not in all this realm a braver knight than you, I entreat you, for the love you bear me, to go upon this journey. Carry my heart with you against the infidels."

The Good Sir James, with tears streaming down his cheeks, promised to do this.

"Then," said the king, "I die in greater ease, for I know that you will do all you have promised."

King Robert died in 1329. In every hamlet there was weeping and lamenting as the sad procession journeyed to Dunfermline. There the king was laid to rest. There, to this day, you can see where lies the Hero-King of Scotland.

"THE HEART OF THE BRUCE"

"Now," says an old teller of tales, "when Sir James Douglas passed with King Robert's heart to fight the infidels, he put it in a silver case. This case was filled also with perfumes and precious ointments. And he took with him Sir William Saint Clair of Roslin, and many another noble knight."

This is how one of them told their adventures:

> " We spoke not as the shore grew less,
>   But gazed in silence back,
> Where the long billows swept away
>   The foam behind our track.

> " And aye we sailed, and aye we sailed,
>   Across the weary sea,
> Until one morn the coast of Spain
>   Rose grimly on our lee."

Now as they drew near the coast of Spain, they heard a clash of arms, and the call of trumpets.

> " The Moors have come from Africa
>   To spoil, and waste, and slay,
> And King Alonzo of Castille
>   Must fight with them to-day.

> " ' Have down, have down,' cried Good Lord James
>   ' Have down into the plain;
> We'll let the Scottish Lion loose
>   Within the fields of Spain! '

> " ' Now welcome to me,' said the king,
>   ' Thou and thy stalwart power;
> Dear is the sight of a Christian knight,
>   Who comes in such an hour! '

> " ' God greet thee well, thou valiant king,
>   Thee and thy belted peers—
> Sir James of Douglas am I called,
>   And these are Scottish spears.'

" ' I know thy name full well, Lord James;
    And honoured may I be,
That those who fought beside the Bruce
    Should fight this day for me!

" ' Take thou the leading of the van,
    And charge the Moors amain;
There is not such a lance as thine
    In all the host of Spain! '

" The Douglas turned towards us then
    Oh, but his glance was high!
' There is not one of all my men
    But is as frank as I.

" ' There is not one of all my knights
    But bears as true a spear—
Then—onwards, Scottish gentlemen,
    And think King Robert's here! '

" The trumpets blew, the cross-bolts flew.
    The arrows flashed like flame,
As, spur in side, and spear in rest,
    Against the foe we came.

" And many a bearded Saracen
    Went down, both horse and man;
For through their ranks we rode like corn,
    So furiously we ran!

" ' Make in! make in! ' Lord Douglas cried—
    ' Make in, my brethren dear
Sir William of St Clair is down;
    We may not leave him here! '

" ' Now Jesu help thee,' said Lord James
    ' Thou kind and true St Clair!
An' if I may not bring thee off,
    I'll die beside thee there! '

" Then in his stirrups up he stood,
    So lion-like and bold
And held the precious heart aloft
    All in its case of gold.

" He flung it from him far ahead,
    And never spake he more,
But—' Pass thou first, thou dauntless heart
    As thou were wont of yore! ' "

Thus fell the " Good Sir James," fighting to the last.

" We lifted thence the Good Lord James,
    And the priceless heart he bore;
And heavily we steered our ship
    Towards the Scottish shore.
" We laid our chief in Douglas Kirk,
    The heart in fair Melrose;
And woeful men were we that day—
    God grant their souls repose! "

From *The Heart of the Bruce*,
by W. E. AYTOUN.

HOW BLACK AGNES KEPT THE CASTLE

David II. was but five years old when he was crowned at Scone. As he was too young to rule, Randolph was chosen regent, or governor, in his stead.

He ruled the land justly, but in his old age he is said to have been cruel. Once he sent soldiers to put some Highland robbers to death.

When they had done so, they placed fifty of their heads round the castle walls. " I like to look on these better than on a garland of roses," said the regent grimly.

Other enemies soon sprang up to trouble the land. In the days of Bruce, many of the Scottish nobles held lands in England. After Bannockburn, they had to choose between England and Scotland. Those who paid homage to England's king lost their lands in Scotland.

By the Treaty of Northampton, Bruce promised to give back these lands to their lords. Some nobles, however, who were too friendly to England, never received them.

When those nobles saw that Scotland had a boy-king, they said to themselves, " Now is the time to win back our estates." With Edward Balliol, a son of John Balliol, as their leader, they landed in Fife. Edward III. of England helped them in secret. At Dupplin Moor, near Perth, the Scots were beaten.

Balliol was then crowned at Scone, and became Edward's " man." It seemed as if Bannockburn had never been won.

Randolph was now dead, but his second son, the Earl of Moray, and Archibald Douglas, brother of Sir James, suddenly attacked Balliol at Annan. He fled to England in such a hurry that he had no time to clothe himself.

So Edward III. thought he would try to win Scotland for himself. He was a great warrior, like his grandfather, the "Hammer of the Scots." At Halidon Hill, near Berwick, he paid the Scots back for Bannockburn.

> "At Bannock Burn were you too keen,
>   But now has Edward wreaked it, I ween."

So sang an English poet.

Balliol and Edward ruled Scotland between them, Edward ruling the country south of the Forth. The Scots sent King David and his queen to France for safety. They had to begin to do the work of Bruce over again.

Many brave deeds were done, but the minstrels never tired of singing of a lady's bravery:—

> "Some sing o' lords, an' some o' knichts,
>   An' some o' michty men o' war,
>   But I sing o' a leddy bricht,
>   The Black Agnace o' Dunnebar."

She was Randolph's daughter, and had married the Earl of March. She was known as "Black Agnes," because of her dark complexion.

One day, her husband left her to keep his castle of Dunbar. While he was away, the English, under the Earl of Salisbury, came to besiege it.

They brought their machines for throwing stones. These were like great see-saws. One

H

end of a huge plank was fixed firmly in the ground. The other was bent down with chains. Then a stone was laid on it, and the chains

suddenly let go. Away sped the stone bullet to its mark. Little did Black Agnes heed such shot. She and her maidens mocked the English. With their napkins, they carefully wiped away from the walls the dust caused by the stones.

Next the English tried another plan. This time they made great wooden turrets, many storeys high, called "sows." Each storey was crowded with men. These sows were rolled on wheels close to the wall. Then the men began to make holes in the wall with their tools. But the brave countess was ready for them. She made her men-at-arms drop a great mass of rock on the moving turret. It crashed through from top to bottom.

Then, as the soldiers fled, her bowmen rained down showers of arrows. One pierced the heart of a knight, through his armour. "Aye," said Salisbury, " Agnes's love-shafts go straight to the heart." The English gave up in despair.

" Came they early, came they late,
    They found Black Agnes at the gate."

WHAT THE FRENCH SAW IN SCOTLAND

The Scots were so successful that they brought their king over from France. He led an army against England, but at Neville's Cross, near Durham, the Scots were defeated.

They had forgotten what the wise Bruce had said on his deathbed. He had told his nobles never to fight in the open, but to make the bogs and hills of their native land their castles.

So once again the English archers won the day. David himself was captured, and for eleven years lay in prison in England.

Moreover, a dreadful and mysterious disease, called the Black Death, came upon Scotland. One out of every three persons died.

King David was at last set free on promising to pay one hundred thousand merks. The Scots grumbled very much at this heavy burden.

David even wrote to Edward, saying that

he would be his vassal, if he did not ask him to pay his ransom of one hundred thousand merks. But, when the Scots heard of this shameful bargain, they were very angry.

It is sad to think that the son of Robert the Bruce could even dream of such a thing. When David died, there were few to mourn his death.

He left no children. Robert the Steward next became king. His mother was a daughter of Robert the Bruce. The Stewards were the officers of the king, who looked after his castles, palaces, and servants. When Robert the Steward got the crown, he called himself Robert Stewart.

He was a noble-looking man, but he had weak eyes. The Scots called him " King Blearie." He was too gentle for those rough times. If he had not had six stalwart sons, he might have fared ill, for he could not keep his nobles in order.

In his day there were many comings and goings between France and Scotland. For the King of England had begun a war with France which lasted a hundred years, and the Scots were always willing to help the French.

In 1385 the French king sent his admiral, Sir John de Vienne, with money and men, to Scotland. The visitors came to Edinburgh, but the king was not there.

They did not think much of Edinburgh.   It

had only four hundred houses. Nor were there any fine palaces, or beautiful rooms, or even " good soft beds." They could get no iron for their horses, nor leather to make harness.

" Let us get to business at once," they grumbled, " and then let us off home again. This is a poor country."

" My fair sirs," said the admiral, " you cannot always be in such a fine town as Paris. Those who wish to live a good life must put up with the good and the bad."

Nor did the Scots like the French either. " Why have they come? " said one. " Can't we manage our own affairs? " said another.

At last King Robert arrived in Edinburgh. The French knights greeted him, and told him that they longed to do some brave deeds of arms.

So they set off with the king's sons and thirty thousand men. When they drew near the English, the French knights were delighted. " Now," said they, " we can show how nobly we of France can fight."

But this time, the Scots kept in mind the advice of the dying Bruce, and began to retreat.

" We are valiant men," said the French angrily, " we never flee." Then Douglas took them to a high hill, and let them see what a great host the English army was. " You are right," was all they said.

The Scots slipped past the English, and won great booty in the wealthy country across the Border.

Meanwhile the English burned and wasted in Scotland, but they did little real damage. The Scots had even removed the straw roofs of their houses, and hidden them. Their cattle were safe in the depths of the forests.

When the French and Scots came back, they found nothing but ruin. Douglas laughingly said, " With six or eight stakes and some turf, there will soon be new houses. The cattle are not far off."

So the French went back to their native land, wondering at what they had seen. They were not very pleased with their visit. The Scots liked French money and armour, but they did not care for strange soldiers in their land.

HOW A DEAD DOUGLAS WON
A FIELD

In spite of King Robert's wishes, the Scottish nobles made up their minds to invade England. They marched south secretly in two bodies. Those who went by the east were commanded by the Earl of Douglas.

By following bypaths, they reached the river Tyne before the English knew of their coming.

Then smoking villages from the Tyne to Durham told the story of their march.

As they returned by Newcastle, they fell in with Lord Henry Percy, son of the Earl of Northumberland. He was called " Hotspur," because he was ever eager to gallop against the foe.

In the fight, Douglas captured Hotspur's lance, with its silk pennon adorned with pearls.

" I will carry it to my Castle of Dalkeith," cried the bold earl, as he bore away the prize. " There I will place it on the highest tower, so that it may be seen afar."

" That you shall never do," said Percy. " I will win it back before you see Scotland again."

" Then you must come this night, and seek it. I shall fix it before my tent door, and see if you will venture to take it away."

But no Hotspur came that night, nor the next. The Scots wended their way homewards, and encamped at Otterburn. Here Douglas, like a true knight, waited three days to see if Hotspur would make good his boast.

At twilight on the third day of waiting, the cry arose in the Scottish camp, " The English are upon us." Though some were supping, and others sleeping, Douglas soon had his men ready for battle.

It was the 19th August 1388. The night was beautiful and calm. The moon shone bright, and the evening breeze blew softly over the gently sloping hills.

"Percy! Percy!" shouted the English, as they threw themselves on the foe.

"Douglas! Douglas!" cried the Scots, as they followed their leader's pennon into the fray.

Never was such a fight fought between English and Scots. No knight turned his back. The stars shone down on moonlit armour and waving lances.

At last the Scots, few in numbers, began to give way. The Scottish earl grasped his battle-axe with both hands. "Douglas! Douglas!" he shouted, as he dashed into the thickest of the fight.

But he was borne to the ground, pierced by three lances. His men did not see him fall. His chaplain, William of North Berwick, fighting fiercely, guarded his body as it lay with the blood-stained pennon beneath.

"How fares it, cousin?" said Sir John Sinclair, as he knelt beside the dying knight.

"Not well. Thanks be to God, but few of my forefathers have died in their beds. Avenge my death. Take my banner. Shout 'Douglas!' Let no one know I die. There is an old saying that a dead Douglas shall win a field. Perchance it may be so this night."

So Sir John raised the tattered flag, and once again the Douglas war-cry was heard. The Scots showed such courage that the English fled.

Hotspur and his brother were taken prisoners. Douglas was laid to rest in Melrose Abbey, with the war-stained flag above his grave. Thus ended the famous battle of Otterburn. A dead Douglas had won the field.

THE STORY OF HAL O' THE WYND

In those far-off times, a fierce and warlike people lived in the Highlands of Scotland, north of the town of Perth. They dwelt together in groups of families, called " clans." Each clan had a chief.

These chiefs were like kings. They made laws, and punished their clansmen if they disobeyed them. As for the King of Scotland, few had ever seen him. The clansmen lived a life full of robbing and fighting, slaying and burning.

In the days of Robert III., who wore the crown of Scotland after his father Robert II., there was a deadly quarrel between two clans. One was called the Clan Chattan, the other the Clan Kay. So fiercely did they wage war on each other, that the whole country was alarmed.

At length, they agreed to fight it out to the death in a tournament before the king. Thirty champions were to be chosen by each clan. Each was to be armed with a sword, a targe or shield, a battle-axe, and a dagger. But no armour was to be worn.

The battle took place at Perth, on a beautiful meadow called the " Inch." The Inch is partly surrounded by the river Tay. Here stands were built for the king and his nobles.

Then, to the sound of the bagpipes, the two clans marched to battle. The Earl Marshal carefully looked to see that each man had the proper weapons. On counting the men on each side, he found that the Clan Chattan had only twenty-nine.

Another man had to be found. The chief promised half a French crown to the one who would fight for him. Hal o' the Wynd, a smith, offered himself. He was very strong, and knew well how to ply his sword.

Raising their war-cries, the two clans now fell on each other furiously. No mercy was shown. The air was filled with the shouts of the onlookers as they watched the savage fight.

In the midst of the struggle, the chief of the Clan Chattan saw Hal standing by.

" Are you afraid? " he asked.

" Not I," said the smith, " but I have done a half-crown's work."

" Fight on," cried the chief, " to him who grudges not to work, I will not grudge wages."

Once again the smith's great sword flashed in the summer sun. At last only one of the Clan Kay, and ten of the Clan Chattan, were left alive. One man could not fight eleven. Plunging into the river, he fled back to his native glen.

It is said that the Highlands were more peaceful after this dreadful day's work.

Meanwhile the king's son was growing up a handsome lad. His father made him Duke of Rothesay. At the same time, the king's brother became Duke of Albany. These were the first Scottish dukes.

When the English laid siege to Edinburgh Castle, the Duke of Rothesay bravely defended it. But Albany, though he had a large army, never came to his nephew's help. He did not like him. Albany wished to be the chief person in Scotland.

Now the Duke of Rothesay, though fair to look upon, was wicked and wild. Albany persuaded the king to shut his son up in Falkland Tower. There he died. Many have thought that Albany caused him to be starved to death.

Even the king did not trust his brother after this. He sent his remaining son, James, to France to be brought up. But one day, word came that the ship he had sailed in had been taken by the English, off Flamborough Head.

Thirteen days later, King Robert III. died of grief. He had a gentle heart, but Scotland needed a sterner king to tame its proud barons.

HOW THEY FOUGHT AT
RED HARLAW

When young Prince James was brought before King Henry of England, he said: " Why did my royal brother of Scotland send his son to France? He can learn French quite as easily here, for I know it pretty well."

This he said in jest, but he kept his word. James learned Latin, and French, and English. Every day he practised with bows and arrows, and was taught how to use his sword. He could also sing, and dance, and play the harp. He even wrote poems.

Meanwhile his uncle Albany ruled Scotland. In his day the Highlanders began to help the English against the King of Scots.

One wild chief was called Donald, Lord of the Isles. He ruled the Hebrides, and even a large part of the mainland. He thought himself as great as the king, and said he should be Earl of Ross. But Albany made his own son, Murdoch, Earl instead.

In revenge, Donald gathered the clansmen. To the Isle of Mull came the Macleods of Skye, the Camerons of Lochaber, and many other Highland clans. They marched to plunder Aberdeen. Burnt hamlets and smoking farms showed where the pitiless clansmen had gone.

Eighteen miles north of Aberdeen, at Harlaw, the Earl of Mar, with a small band of knights and the townsmen of Aberdeen, met the Lord of the Isles. From morn till night the battle raged.

The Highlanders leapt on the knights' backs, and stabbed them between the joints of their armour; or else they dragged them from their horses, and dirked them.

When night fell, the flower of the Lowlanders and thousands of the Highlanders were "sleeping at Red Harlaw." Next day the clans slipped back to their hills. Mar and his men had won the day.

This battle showed that the Lowlanders and not the Highlanders, were to be the rulers of Scotland. For many a long year the battle was remembered. The boys used to play at Harlaw in their games.

Albany died in 1420. His son, Murdoch, ruled till 1424. In that year King James I. was set free, after promising to pay a large ransom.

He brought home an English wife. In a poem he tells how first he saw her. One day, sad at heart, he looked out of his prison window. Round about grew beautiful flowers in a garden where nightingales sang the livelong night. There he saw a lady fairer than the loveliest flower. When she had gone, the king vowed to himself she should be his wife.

When he was set free, he married her. As she was a relation of Henry of England, it was thought that now there would be no war between the two countries.

James I. wished for peace. First of all he had to pay his ransom to King Henry. Then he had to tame his proud nobles, who had been too long without a king to keep them in order.

Murdoch was the first to suffer, for the king thought that he had not been anxious enough to bring his king home again.

Every year the wise men of the land met in Parliament to make laws. These were now written in the Scots language, so that all could understand them.

All men were to shoot with the bow every week. James hoped to make the Scots as good archers as the English.

The forests were not to be cut down, for wood was becoming scarce. Salmon were not to be caught in the rivers for three years. Only the rich were to wear furs. Clothes were to have " narrow sleeves and little pockets."

Then James took away the estates of the barons who would not obey him. The nobles began to feel that the king was too strict.

They began to plot to murder the king. Sir Robert Graham was their leader. He fled to the hills, and waited for revenge.

THE MURDER OF A KING

Now the king wished to spend Christmas of the year 1436 at Perth. So he and a number of lords and ladies rode northwards, and came to the shores of the Forth, after the sun had sunk in the west.

In the dim twilight, a Highland woman, tattered and old, rose suddenly before them.

"Beware! beware! my lord the king," she cried, "for unless you turn back, there is no way for you but death."

But the king and his company passed over, and came to Perth. There they stayed at the monastery, for the castle was being repaired. The nights passed in feasting and merriment.

One evening the lords and ladies were all together. After they had played chess together, the king took his harp, and sang of how he had won his bride.

As the song ended, a loud knock was heard at the gate. It was the weird woman, who had come again to warn the king. But he would not see her, for the hour was late. So she fled into the darkness, crying, "Woe! woe! the thing must be."

All retired to rest. The last to go was Sir Robert Stewart, who was a traitor. He had taken away all the bolts of the doors, so that they could not be shut. He had placed planks across the ditch surrounding the monastery. Graham was hiding in the garden with three hundred men.

Now, as the king talked with the queen, suddenly there was a glare of torches and a clash of steel. They guessed who came thus by night.

The queen and her ladies sprang to bolt the doors. Alas! no bars were there. The king snatched the tongs from the chimney-nook. With them he tore up a plank in the floor, and let himself down into the vault beneath. He might have escaped, but only three days before he had closed up the way out, because, when he played tennis, he lost his balls there.

In the meantime, the queen and her ladies tried to make the floor look smooth again. Before all was ready, the tramp of armed men came near!

It was then, it is said, that one of the ladies, Catherine Douglas, rushed to the door, and thrust her arm through in place of the bar. The frail white arm could hold them back but a few minutes.

" 'Twas Catherine Douglas sprang to the door,
But I fell back Kate Barlass."

The traitors pressed into the hall. In every nook and cranny they searched for the king.

I

One of them would even have stabbed the queen; but Graham's son said, "This is a woman, we seek the king."

James could not be found, so they left the monastery. Just as the king was getting ready to return, the murderers came back. They had remembered the vault beneath. Now they noticed the tell-tale plank half-raised.

As they peered down, they saw the king half undressed. With drawn sword, one leaped down. The king caught him and threw him. A second

met the same end. The king was manly and strong, and fought fiercely for his life.

At last three sprang down. "Mercy," cried the king.

"Tyrant," said Graham. "You never gave mercy, you shall have none now." Saying this, he struck the king, so that he fell. Sixteen wounds were found in the poet-king's breast.

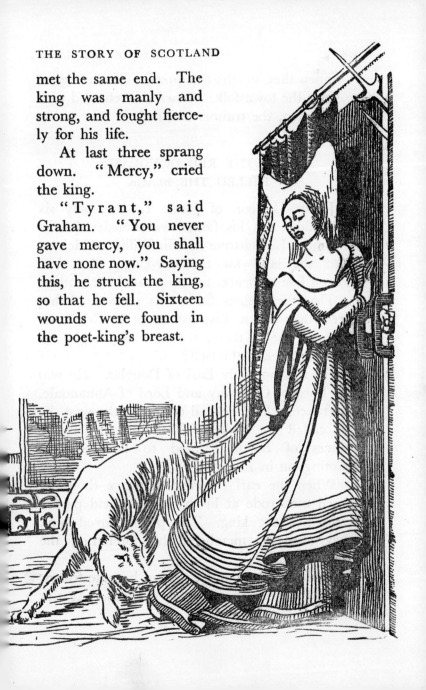

Then they sought the queen. She had gone to warn the townsfolk. When she returned with armed men, the traitors had fled.

HOW THE RED DOUGLASES KILLED THE BLACK

James II., son of James I., was only six years old when his father was murdered. Sir Alexander Livingstone and Sir William Crichton ruled the land for the boy-king. But they did not live at peace, for they hated each other.

The other nobles did as they pleased. What cared they for a Livingstone or a Crichton? Was not one of them, the Earl of Douglas, as great as the king himself?

He was not only Earl of Douglas. He was also Lord of Galloway and Lord of Annandale. In France, where he had estates in the west, he was called the Duke of Touraine, just as the Princes of Scotland used to be Earls of Huntingdon in England.

When the earl travelled about, a thousand armed men rode at his back. He held parliaments like the king. The people loved him. They always remembered his forefather, the Good Sir James.

So Livingstone and Crichton became friends to try to tame the Earl of Douglas. At this time he was but a lad of sixteen. The two plotters asked him and his brother, with fair words, to come and see the nine-year-old king. The three lads soon got to like one another.

But one day, as they were at dinner, a black bull's head was placed on the table. Pale with fear, the Douglases tried to escape, for they knew it was a sign of death.

In vain the king begged Livingstone and Crichton to let his new friends go free. Armed men seized them. Soon after, they were put to death in the court of the castle. "The Black Dinner," as it was called, was never forgotten.

> " Edinburgh Castle, town and tower,
>   God grant you sink for sin!
>   And that even for the black dinner
>   Earl Douglas got therein."

James the Fat, the next Earl of Douglas, was very lazy. When he died, his son, William, became earl. He was a daring warrior, like his forefather who fought at Otterburn.

The king was now old enough to rule. At first, he and Douglas were very friendly, but Scotland was too small a country for two great men like the king and Douglas.

The earl began to help the king's enemies, so James wrote a letter to him with his own hand, asking him to come and talk with him.

He promised that not a hair of his head would be touched.

Douglas rode boldly into Stirling. There he and the king supped together. Then they began to talk.

"You have made a bond with my enemies," said James to the earl. "You must break it."

"Nay," said Douglas, "I neither can nor will."

In a fit of anger, James drove his dagger into Douglas's body. "If you will not, this shall," said he.

All the friends of Douglas gathered to avenge his death. James, the brother of the murdered earl, tied the king's letter of safety to his horse, and dragged it through the streets of Stirling.

STIRLING CASTLE

Twenty-four of his trumpeters blew a blast, to show that he was no longer the king's vassal. Then he burned the town.

For more than three years the quarrel lasted. But, in the end, the earl was defeated, and forced to flee to England. The Douglases were tamed.

James II. gave some of their estates to the Earl of Angus, whose family was called the Red Douglases. It was said, " The Red Douglases have killed the Black Douglases."

HOW SCOTLAND GREW

There was now a real king in Scotland— King James II. He ruled Scotland well for five years, and his people loved him. He used to wander about from place to place, visiting the country folk in their farms.

When he was with his army, he would walk among his soldiers and sit down beside them. Then he ate and drank with them. He was a true soldier-king, and liked to lead his army to battle.

About this time, the nobles of England were very unruly. They were always quarrelling among themselves, and with the king. James thought it would be a good time to try to take the Castle of Roxburgh. Since the battle of Neville's Cross, when David II. was king, it had been held by the English.

The castle had very strong walls. To break them down, James used cannon. These were the first to be fired in Scotland. They were made of pieces of iron, with hoops to keep them tight. The hoops were made firm with wedges.

Now the king was very anxious to know all about these new war-machines. One Sunday morning, as he was watching them being fired, one of them burst. The king was killed. His brave wife bade the soldiers not give in, and shortly afterwards the castle was taken.

Once again Scotland had a boy-king. James III. was only ten years of age when he was crowned in Kelso Abbey, on the 10th August 1460.

Bishop Kennedy was made regent. He ruled for five years. This bishop was very clever. As we have seen, there was much fighting in England at this time. The King of England wanted the Scots to help him. But Bishop Kennedy only promised to do so, if the King of England gave up the town of Berwick on the Tweed.

When James grew up, he married Margaret, a daughter of Christian, King of Norway and

Denmark. Christian said he would give his daughter a large sum of money when she became Queen of Scotland. But he had not enough money, so he gave King James the Orkney and Shetland Islands instead.

Roxburgh, Berwick, and these islands now belonged to the King of Scots. Scotland was a bigger country than it had ever been before. Yet James III. was not a great king.

First of all, his barons did not admire him. He was not a soldier-king like his father. He liked books and pictures, fine churches, and beautiful music.

Most of the barons could not even read or write. The friends the king liked best were Cochrane, an architect; Roger, a musician; and Hommyle, a tailor. The proud nobles hated the " mason " and " fiddler," as they called Cochrane and Roger.

The king's two brothers, the Earl of Albany and the Earl of Mar, were the men for those warlike times. They were bold horsemen and fierce fighters.

Soon a quarrel arose between the king and his brothers. Mar was put in prison, where he died soon after. Albany fled to England.

Then James III. quarrelled with his nobles. They said the king was too fond of Cochrane and Roger, and other low-born favourites.

HOW ARCHIBALD DOUGLAS
BELLED THE CAT

About this time, the French asked the King of Scotland to help them against the English. So James led an army from Edinburgh, and came to the town of Lauder, on the Leader, a tributary of the Tweed.

He took with him all his favourites, the fiddler, the mason, the tailor, and many others. The proud nobles thought that now was the time to get rid of them.

They met in the church to see what was to be done. There Lord Gray stood up, and told them this story:—

" My friends," said he, " the mice once held a meeting to see how they could save themselves from the cat. One mouse said, ' Why not put a bell round the cat's neck? Then we shall know when he comes.' ' Yes,' said another, ' that is a very nice plan, but who will put the bell on the cat?' "

Lord Gray sat down. All the nobles looked at one another. " Ah! I see," said Archibald, Earl of Angus. " I'll bell the cat." Ever afterwards he was called Archibald Bell-the-Cat.

Just at that moment, a knock was heard at the door. The door was opened and Cochrane entered. He was beautifully dressed in a black velvet hunting suit. Round his neck he wore a chain of gold. At his side was a hunting-horn covered with precious stones.

Angus went up to him and snatched away the golden chain. " A halter to hang you would suit you better."

Another pulled the horn from his belt. " You have hunted mischief long enough," said he.

" Is this in fun, or in earnest? " asked Cochrane. " It is in earnest, as you will soon see," was the answer.

Then the other favourites were seized also. On Lauder Bridge they were all hanged in a row. Cochrane begged for a silken rope, because he was an earl, but he was hanged with one of horse-hair instead.

The nobles led the king back to Edinburgh, and kept him prisoner in the castle. But he was soon free again. A new company of favourites were always beside him. The barons hated their king more than ever. Would he not take vengeance on them for what they had done at Lauder Bridge?

Once more they met together, but this time they had an army with them. They marched to Stirling Castle, where Prince James, the king's son, was kept by the governor. They forced him to give up the prince to them.

Then at Sauchieburn, about a mile from Bannockburn, they met the army of King James. The king had never been a soldier, but that day he rode a great war-horse. At his side he wore the sword which Robert the Bruce had used on the famous battlefield.

But King James was not so brave as King Robert. His horse bore him from the fight. As he fled, he came to a mill near the Bannock Burn. The miller's wife, it is said, was filling a pitcher at the stream. As the horse galloped past, it shied, and the king fell heavily to the ground.

He was carried into the miller's house. " Who are you? " asked the miller's wife, as he began to open his eyes again. " This morn, I was your king," he sighed.

Rushing out of doors, the woman cried, " A priest, a priest for the king." A stranger was passing by. " I am a priest," said he. Joyfully the woman led him to the king. He bent over him. " Are you about to die? " asked he.

" I know not; but I should like to confess my sins, and be pardoned," answered the king.

" This will give you pardon," said the man, stabbing his king to the heart. This happened in 1488, twenty-eight years after James had been crowned.

THE STORY OF BOLD SIR
ANDREW WOOD

After the battle, word came to Prince James' who became James IV., that his father was in the ship of Sir Andrew Wood of Largo. The nobles sent to see if it were true. But the messenger came back saying that the king was not on board.

Then they sent for the bold seaman himself. He was very cunning. " I cannot come," said he, " unless two of your friends stay in my ship while I am on land. If you harm me, then my sailors will hang these friends of yours." The bargain was made, and Sir Andrew Wood came ashore at Leith.

" Is not the king in your ship? " said the lords. " I wish he were, with all my heart; I should defend him from traitors," said Sir Andrew.

So the lords went away, ashamed to hear the truth from a brave man's lips. Afterwards they bade Andrew Barton, another bold sailor, attack Sir Andrew Wood.

" Why," said he, " not ten ships in Scotland could attack that sea-rover. He is too good a mariner."

It was not long before they were very pleased to ask Sir Andrew to help them. The ships of the King of England came sailing into the Firth of Forth, and captured many Scottish ships and men.

Then King James IV. sent to his great captain. He bade him go forth to sea and fight the English. So Sir Andrew sailed with his two ships, the " Yellow Carvel," and the " Flower." Near Dunbar, he took five English ships. He brought them and their captains to Leith.

Now when the King of England heard of this, he was very angry. He sent word through all his kingdom, promising a great sum of money to the one who would capture the Scottish captain.

It was then that " Stephen Bull took in hand to pass to the sea, and fight Sir Andrew, and bring him prisoner to the King of England, either dead or alive."

With three great ships of war, he came up the Firth of Forth. At the back of the Isle of May he lay in wait. There he captured some fishermen. He would not let them go till they had shown him Sir Andrew Wood.

" One summer morn, a little after daybreak," two ships were seen off St Abb's Head. The Scottish sailors were sent to the top of the mast to spy if it was Sir Andrew Wood or not. At first they would not tell, but at

last they said, " These are the ships of our
king."

Stephen Bull and his men were right merry
to hear the news.   The wine was brought forth.
Many a cup they drank to cheer their hearts.
Then each man went to his post.

Now Sir Andrew drew near.   When he saw
the English ships, he said : " Let us not be afraid.
These men have come to take us, but please God,
they shall fail.   Let the gunners be in their places.
Fill the rigging with the archers.   Have ready the
hand fire-balls to throw into the enemy's ships.
See that each man in the forecastle has a sharp
two-edged sword.   Let every one be bold for his
king and country."

" By this time, the sun rose and shone bright
upon the sails."   The English ships were great
and high.   They were called " galleys."   But
the Scots did not lose heart.   They boldly sailed
close, and tied their ships fast to the English
galleys.

From the rising to the setting sun the fight
raged.   The country folk along the shore watched
the battle, " terrible to see."

As night fell, they parted.   On the morrow,
the day broke fair.   On every side the trumpets
blew, as the two captains led their men once more
into the fray.

So fiercely did they fight, that they knew not

that the tide was taking them far out to sea. Thus they came to the Inchcape Rock.

When the Scots saw how far they had come, they " doubled their strokes upon the English." Stephen Bull and his men were captured, and taken to Dundee.

Then King James rewarded Sir Andrew richly. He sent Stephen Bull and his men home again to the King of England with this message: " I have as brave men," said he, " by sea and land in Scotland, as there are in England. Send no more captains to disturb my realm; if you do, I shall not treat them so well next time."

Like the good King Robert, James IV. loved the sea. He spent many an hour upon the waves. He cut down almost all the woods in Fife, to build a ship, the " Great Michael."

It was built at Newhaven, near Leith, and was to be the largest ship afloat.

Timber was even brought from Norway. All the carpenters in Scotland worked at it, and many from lands across the sea. Never was seen such a huge sea-monster.

When it was got to sea, James went aboard. At the mast-head flew the Scottish Lion.

The "Great Michael"

Then the king did a strange thing. He ordered a shot to be fired at the "Great Michael." The bullet struck, but the ship was not harmed. Its walls were ten feet thick.

James IV. built many other ships. For this reason he has been called the "Founder of the Scottish Navy."

K

THE STORY OF THE THISTLE
AND THE ROSE

It was a long time since the Scots had had a king they loved so well. This is what a Spaniard said about James IV.:—

" He is a noble-looking man, neither tall nor short. He never cuts his hair nor his beard. He is very pious. He does not eat meat on Wednesdays nor Fridays, for these are holy days.

" He gives much to the poor. He is very severe, especially to murderers. He likes war. When he is not fighting, he hunts in the mountains."

Sometimes the king used to disappear for days. Then he would be found in a little church in some out-of-the-way place, praying for pardon for his father's death.

To show how sorry he was for this dreadful deed, he used to wear an iron belt. Every year he made it heavier.

James liked ships and sailors, but he also cared for books and scholars. During his reign, the first books were printed in Scotland. A law was also made that the children of the barons were to be sent to school when they were eight years of age.

Now the kings of lands across the sea, the Kings of France and of Spain, of Norway and of Denmark, heard of this noble prince. All wished to have the King of Scotland as their friend.

But the most anxious of all was Henry VII. of England. In 1502 it was agreed that his daughter, Margaret, should marry James. " Now," it was thought, " there will be peace between the two kingdoms."

It was in July 1503, that Margaret crossed the Border to see the land that was to be her home. With her journeyed the Earl of Surrey and other attendants. Never had they looked on a fairer scene. The sun, as if to welcome the princess, shone bright on the ripening fields of barley and oats, peas and beans.

There were no hedges, in those days, to divide these fertile lands from one another. Often the noble company had to climb the hill slopes to pass lochs, now long since disappeared.

As they drew near Haddington, they rode through the orchards they had heard so much about. Near the town itself, they visited its famous church, the " Lamp of the Lothians."

When they reached Dalkeith, the king was waiting to greet his lady. Next day, they came to Edinburgh. Its townsfolk had been busy getting everything ready. They were very proud of their city. It was now the chief town, or capital, of Scotland.

Travellers from afar said that nowhere in the wide world was there such a fine street as the High Street. It had beautiful stone houses. The fronts were made of wood. Each house had a wooden gallery, or balcony, on the outside of the first storey.

This must have made the street look narrow, though, in those days, it was thought to be very wide. It was even paved with rough stones; but it was very dirty. The dung-heaps were in the very street itself, and scores of pigs roamed about just as they liked.

Of course, days before Margaret drew near, the town bellman had been sent round the city. Everyone was ordered to make his part of the street clean and tidy.

In front of the city gate, a wooden arch had been erected. It had two towers and three windows. These windows were filled with pretty children, dressed as angels. When the king and his lady passed beneath, the middle window opened. One of the angels came down, and gave the princess the keys of the city.

Every balcony was crowded. The bells rang merrily. Beautiful tapestries were swinging in the breeze. What is that the king is pointing out to Margaret?

It is a lovely piece of cloth. On it are seen the Red Rose of England and the Thistle of Scotland twining round each other. Farther down the street, they pass the Cross. Near it is the Fountain. On this glad day it runs wine. At last, Holyrood Palace is reached.

In the Abbey, James and Margaret were married next day. It was the Union of the Thistle and the Rose. Exactly one hundred years later, their great-grandson became king both of England and Scotland.

HOW "THE FLOWERS O' THE FOREST WERE A' WEDE AWA'"

For ten years after his marriage, James ruled over Scotland. Far and near he travelled. Even in the north, the fierce clansmen saw their king, and learned to obey him.

Though there was peace at home, there was a continual quarrel with the King of England. It seemed as if the Union of the Thistle and the Rose had been forgotten.

The wild men of the Borders were always fighting. On the sea, Andrew Barton and Sir Andrew Wood took many an English galley. Each king blamed the other for these misdeeds.

At this time, also, the King of France was at war with the King of England. The Scots, since the days of Balliol, had liked the French better than the English.

For all these reasons the two kings went to war. But many strange things took place before James IV. went over the Border.

Once he was praying in Linlithgow Church. "There came in a man clad in a blue gown." When he came to where the king was sitting, he spake thus:—

> "My mother sent me from afar,
> Sir King, to warn thee not to war,—

> Woe waits on thine array;
> James Stewart, doubly warned, beware:
> God keep thee as He may!"

Thereupon, " he vanished like a blink of the sun."

When the king came to Edinburgh, a voice was heard at midnight at the town cross. It cried out the names of those who would fall in battle.

Yet the king heeded not. He gathered the greatest army ever seen in Scotland. Here came the clansmen of the Highlands, the Borderers, the burghers, the yeomen, and the archers of Ettrick—the Flowers o' the Forest.

It was in August 1513, that James passed south. On his way he took Norham Castle, where, in the olden days, Edward I. had given the Scottish crown to John Balliol.

Meanwhile, the Earl of Surrey was again on the road to Scotland. This time he was not a messenger of peace. No royal lady did he bring with him, but the pick of English warriors.

As he drew near the Scots, he found them on Flodden Hill, with the river Till beneath. They were not eager for the fray. The weather was windy, and wet, and cold. The Scots had gained much booty on the road, and would gladly have been safe at home again.

A message came from Surrey. " If you are a true knight," said he to King James, " come down into the plain and let us fight like men." " Nay," said the king, " it is I who choose the field at pleasure."

So Surrey passed north, and crossed the Till at Twisel Bridge. Thus he got between the Scots and their native land. Then he marched south again.

When James perceived this, he ordered all the tents to be burned. Hidden by the smoke, the Scots marched to meet the foe.

As Surrey, sitting in his chariot, watched the strife, he saw one wing of the Scots give way. The English rushed off in pursuit.

Then they came back, and took the Scots in the rear. Round the King of Scots, fighting on foot, were gathered the bravest of his men. One by one they fell as the English arrows pierced their armour. The ground, wet with rain, was drenched with blood.

> " O Douglas for thy leading wand!
> Fierce Randolph for thy speed!
> O for one hour of Wallace wight,
> Or well-skilled Bruce, to rule the fight,
> Another sight had seen that morn,
> And Flodden had been Bannockburn! "

But it was not to be. In vain the Scots took off their shoes to fight more firmly on the slippery ground. In vain the king's battle hammer, or mace, rose and fell, dealing death at every blow.

The shades of evening fell on that gallant ring still struggling to the last. In the centre lay Scotland's king, pierced by two arrows. Round him lay thirteen earls, twelve lords, and hundreds of knights.

The Flowers o' the Forest were a' wede awa'.

THE STORY OF A BORDER REIVER

These were gloomy days for Scotland. In every house, rich or poor, there was grief for the loved ones who lay dead on Flodden Field.

> " That day made many a fatherless child,
>   And many a widow poor,
>   And many a Scottish gay lady
>   Sat weeping in her bower."

There was little time for such sorrow. The English might be upon them at any moment.

Quickly the burghers of Edinburgh built a wall to protect their city.

Everybody lent a hand. As you look at parts of it to-day, you can see that few masons helped to build it. But the English never came, for they, too, had lost their bravest on that fatal day.

Once more a regent had to be chosen, for James V. was only an infant. At first, Margaret, the widow of James IV., ruled the land. During this time, she married Douglas, Earl of Angus. This displeased the other nobles.

They invited the Duke of Albany to come home from France. He was the son of James III.'s brother, but he had lived so long in France that he was almost a Frenchman.

There were now two parties in Scotland. There were those who liked Albany and his friend the Earl of Arran. The others wished the queen and the Earl of Angus to rule over them.

The party of Albany wanted to help the French. Queen Margaret, being the sister of Henry VIII. of England, wished Scotland to be the friend of England.

There was continual fighting between the two factions, the Hamiltons, or Albany's friends, and the Douglases, or the queen's friends. Once their men-at-arms met in Edinburgh. In a moment the swords were drawn, and fighting began.

Gavin Douglas went to Archbishop Beaton, and asked him to put an end to the fray. " Upon my conscience," said the priest, striking his breast, " I cannot."

" Your conscience clatters," said Douglas,

as he heard the rattle of armour beneath the priest's robes. So the fight in the streets went on. The Douglases "cleared the causeway" of the Hamiltons, as the townsfolk said in those days.

At last Albany, tired of trying to rule such lawless men, returned to France. Douglas and the queen now said that James was old enough to rule the land himself.

They said so, but he was really a prisoner in Falkland Palace, in Fife. There he lived very quietly. When he was seventeen years of age, he made up his mind to be a real king. One fine morning he escaped, dressed in the clothes of Jockie, the stable-boy.

He reached Stirling Castle. Thence he sent a messenger, ordering the Douglases never to come near him, on pain of death. " Scotland cannot hold us both," said James. The Red Douglases had fallen like the Black.

James V. now began to rule in earnest. There was much to do. During these family quarrels, the barons had no one to keep them in order.

In the Borders, they lived like kings. They dwelt together in families — the Kers, the Maxwells, the Johnstones, the Buccleuchs, and boldest of all, the Armstrongs.

They made all the farmers round about pay

them an extra rent. If they refused, they awoke some fine night to find their farms in flames, and a cry of " A Ker! a Ker! " or " A Johnstone! a Johnstone! " at their doors.

With a bag of oatmeal tied to their saddles, the Borderers roamed about for days, robbing wherever they went. At nightfall, they made their bannocks, and cooked them over the camp fire.

Strange stories are told about some of these bold " reivers," as they were called. Once a Border laird heard an old woman say, " Drive out the laird's coo." " The laird's *coo*," said the reiver, " has it come to that. By my faith, they shall soon say *kye*."

Sure enough, next day he and his men might have been seen driving home a fine herd of cattle. Of course, they had taken them from some of their enemies.

On their way they passed a large haystack. It was the very thing they needed for the cattle. " Ah," said the old rascal, " had ye but four feet ye shouldna' stan' lang there."

These were the lawless men James had to force to obey the laws of the land.

HOW JOHNNIE ARMSTRONG
WAS HANGED AT CARLINRIGG

In 1530 James V. ordered his nobles to gather at Edinburgh for a hunt. They were to bring their hawks and their hounds. But James really wished to hunt men. A poet tells us what happened when they reached the Borders:—

" The king he writes a loving letter,
  With his ain hand sae tenderly;
And he has sent it to Johnnie Armstrong,
  To come and speak with him speedily.

" When Johnnie came before the king,
  Wi' a' his men sae brave to see;
The king he movit his bonnet to him,
  He ween'd he was a king as weel as he.

" ' May I find grace my lord the king,
  Grace for my loyal men and me?
For my name it is Johnnie Armstrong,
  And subject of yours, my lord,' said he.

" ' Awa', awa', thou traitor strong!
  Out o' my sicht soon mayst thou be!
I granted never a traitor's life,
  And now I'll not begin wi' thee!'

" ' Grant me my life, my lord, my king!
  And a brave gift I'll gie to thee;
All between here and Newcastle town
  Shall pay their yearly rent to thee.'

" ' Awa', awa', thou traitor strong!
    Out o' my sicht soon mayst thou be!
I never granted a traitor's life,
    And now I'll not begin wi' thee! '

" ' Ah, had I kenn'd, ere I cam' frae hame,
    How thou unkind wadst be to me,
I would have keepit the Borderside,
    In spite of all thy force and thee.'

" John murdered was at Carlinrigg,
    And all his gallant companie;
But Scotland's heart was never sae wae,
    To see sae mony brave men die.

" Because they saved their countrie deir
    Frae Englishmen: nane were sae bauld;
While Johnnie lived on the Borderside,
    Nane o' them durst come near his hauld."

HOW JOCK HOWIESON WENT
TO SEE THE KING

James V., like several of the former kings, loved to wander about the country. He used to dress like a farmer. In this way he learned many things about the common people, who called him the " King o' the Commons."

He had many adventures. One day he was passing the farm of Braehead, at Cramond Brig, near Edinburgh. Four robbers fell upon him. The king drew his sword and defended himself.

A servant, who was threshing in the barn, heard the clash of arms. Flail in hand, he rushed out to help the traveller. Soon the four thieves were put to flight.

Then the man took the king into the farm-house. He gave him a towel and a basin of water to wash his hands and face. " Who are you? " he asked the king. " I am the Goodman o' Ballengeich," said James.

Then the labourer told the Goodman that he was Jock Howieson, a servant on the farm. " Is there anything you would like very much? " asked the king. " Oh yes," replied Jock, " I should like to have a farm of my own."

Before they parted, the Goodman asked Jock to come and see him at Holyrood Palace. " For

I am also a servant," said he, " but a servant of the king."

Not many days after, Jock Howieson, in his best Sunday clothes, arrived at the palace gates. The king had told the watchers to bring him in at once.

Jock found his friend dressed in the same way as before. Together they visited all the splendid rooms of the palace. We may be sure that Jock thought that nothing could be finer.

" Would you like to see the king? " asked the Goodman. " Oh yes, if you think he would not be angry," said the countryman. " Not at all," said his friend. " But how shall I know the king? " said Jock. " That will be very easy. Only the king will wear his bonnet."

Then they entered the great hall, where all the nobles of the land stood round. In vain the simple man looked for his king.

" Where is the king? " he asked at length. " Didn't I tell you that he would have on his bonnet," said his friend.

" Well," said Jock, " it must be either you or I. We are the only ones with bonnets on our heads."

The king laughed heartily at Jock's idea. Before he left, he was Laird o' the Braehead Farm. Instead of paying rent for it, he was always to have ready a basin and a ewer for the king, whenever he passed over Cramond Brig.

Three hundred years later, a certain John Howieson offered King George IV. a silver basin and ewer when he visited Scotland.

James was never happier than when he was among such simple folk. As for his barons, they did not like him.

His uncle, Henry of England, was always meddling with the affairs of Scotland. He wanted James to change his religion, as he had done. So he asked the King of Scots to meet him at York to talk over the matter. But the Scottish nobles warned James not to go.

Henry was angry at his refusal, and war began. The English crossed the Cheviots. James marched to Fala Hill, about fifteen miles from Edinburgh. Word came that the English were off home again. Not another mile would the nobles of Scotland march towards the Border.

Sad at heart, James led them back to Edinburgh. Afterwards, he sent another army south. Its leader was Sir Oliver Sinclair, a man hated by the great lords of the kingdom.

When the English fell upon them at Solway Moss, they had no heart for fight. They fled by a narrow ford across the river Esk. Only twenty were slain, but hundreds were drowned. Many were taken prisoners.

The king could bear no more sorrow. As he lay dying at Falkland Palace, in Fife, the news arrived that a daughter had been born to him. That daughter was afterwards called Mary, Queen of Scots.

" It cam' wi' a lass, and it will gang wi' a lass," said the unhappy James. He was thinking of Robert II., the son of Marjory, Robert the Bruce's daughter. This Robert was the first Stewart to wear the crown. The dying king thought his new-born daughter would be the last to do so. What he feared, as we shall see, did not come to pass.

HOW THE ENGLISH WOOED
THE QUEEN OF SCOTS

In those far-off times, about four hundred years ago, all the people in Scotland were Roman Catholics. Even the kings of Scotland obeyed the Pope, who lived in Rome, in Italy. He told all men how they were to worship God.

In the days of James V., some people began to long for a change. Many could now read the Bible. They began to think that the Pope asked them to do many things that were not in the Bible.

James IV., you remember, did not eat meat

on Wednesdays or Fridays, because he was a good Roman Catholic.

Then it was said that the priests did not do their duty. Many of them did not visit the sick and the poor. Instead of giving money to the helpless, they rather robbed them.

Those who wished to change all this were called " Reformers," or " Protestants." They said they did not need the Pope to tell them how to worship God.

It was not safe to be a Protestant. The law said that all Protestants were to be burned. Many became Protestants in secret. By and by, more joined them. So it came to pass that, when Mary was the Infant Queen, the regent, the Earl of Arran, was a Protestant.

His enemy was the mother of the queen, a Frenchwoman, called Mary of Lorraine. She and Cardinal Beaton were the leaders of the Roman Catholics.

It happened that the King of England, Henry VIII., had become a Protestant before this time. He had a son, Edward, six years of age.

So he said to himself, " The Regent of Scotland is a Protestant like myself. Now is the time to try to make Scotland and England one."

He asked the Scots to promise that Mary, when she grew up, would be married to his son.

Arran and his friends agreed, and everything was arranged.

But Henry VIII. was a very clever man. He was like Edward I. He really wished to be the overlord of Scotland. To bring this about, he began by asking the Scots to send their queen to England to be brought up at his court.

The Scots were wary. They said their queen would stay with them till she was ten years old. Then the queen-mother and the Cardinal began to say, " It would be far better to trust our old friends, the French. The King of England does not really love the Scots as they do."

Many thought this was quite true. They were much pleased when the Cardinal removed their queen from Linlithgow to Stirling Castle. Might not Henry come, and take her away by force?

When Henry heard what was taking place, he vowed he would force the Scots to do as he wished. He sent the Earl of Hertford, with a fleet of two hundred ships, against the Scots. They came up the Firth of Forth.

Then landing, they drove the townsfolk out of Edinburgh and Leith. For three days and three nights these towns blazed. The English marched home by land, leaving behind them a long line of smoking villages from Musselburgh to Dunbar.

In 1545 the Scots had their revenge. At Ancrum Moor, the English leaders were left dead upon the battlefield.

Again Hertford crossed the Cheviots. He made up a list of his doings in Scotland, and sent it to Henry. He was just like a merchant putting down his bills in his account-book or ledger. Five towns, two hundred and forty-three villages, as well as several beautiful abbeys, had been burned. This was called the " Bloody Ledger."

Even when Henry died, the war still went on. In 1547 the Scots were completely defeated at Pinkie Cleugh, near Musselburgh. Fifteen hundred prisoners were taken; ten thousand were slain. It was long ere this " Black Saturday " was forgotten.

Where was the young queen all this time? She was safe in an island home in the Lake of Menteith, in Perthshire. Here she played with her four Maries—Mary Beaton, Mary Seton, Mary Livingston, and Mary Fleming.

The Scots had had enough of the English " wooing." They sent Queen Mary, now six years of age, to France. It was agreed that she should marry the son of the King of France when she was old enough.

THE STORY OF JOHN KNOX

Now there lived in Scotland, about this time,  a man called John Knox. He was born in Haddington, the country of pleasant orchards and beautiful churches.

When he was a boy, he went to school. A queer place school must have been in those days! All the scholars were together in one room. They sat on the straw-covered floor, which was never very clean.

" Instead of windows, there were holes in the wall. When it was cold or wet, these were filled with cloths. As the scholars went to school very early in the morning, they had to bring little lamps with them."

He must have learned his Latin well, for he went afterwards to the university. A university is a sort of school for grown-up folk. When he left the university, he became a priest and a teacher.

Now there came to Scotland one called George Wishart. He was a Protestant. His delight was to go about the country, preaching to the people. He used to tell them why he had changed his religion.

This of course was against the law, and the queen-mother and Cardinal Beaton were very anxious to put him to death. Wishart knew this, and had always a friend beside him to help him.

Once John Knox was his companion. That night, as the two friends were going home, Wishart said to Knox, " Return to your scholars. One is enough to die."

Knox refused, but at last the two friends said farewell. Knox never saw his bold companion again. That very night, Wishart was seized. He was burned at St Andrews according to the law. Cardinal Beaton watched the scene from his window.

In revenge, the Cardinal himself was killed two months later. It was a cruel deed, as cruel as Wishart's death. In those days it was thought to be quite right to get rid of enemies in this way. Even Knox said that it was " a godly deed."

He had now to flee for refuge to the Castle of St Andrews, where the murderers of Cardinal Beaton had shut themselves up. But the castle was besieged, and French soldiers were sent to help. The castle was taken, and Knox and his friends were made prisoners.

They were not put to death. One morning the jailor brought each man a new suit of clothes. The jacket was made of canvas. It had no sleeves, only holes for the arms. Each man had a little cap to cover his closely cropped hair.

Then they were taken aboard French ships or " galleys." They were now galley-slaves. Chained to the oar, they had to row for months and months, for years and years. An officer, with a heavy whip, stood over them to keep them at their work.

For two long dreary years Knox toiled at the oar. Once, as he looked through the oar-hole, he saw the steeple of his church at St Andrews. " I once preached there," he said to his comrade chained beside him, " and, please God, I shall do so again."

He never lost heart. At last he was set free, but he dared not return to Scotland. For ten years he roamed in foreign lands, teaching and preaching.

During this time, Mary of Lorraine ruled the land for the girl-queen who was in France. She was not very well liked. She was always sending for some of her French friends. To them she gave money and fine estates. They helped her to rule the land.

The Scots began to fear that Scotland would soon be just a part of France. Many who loved their country joined the Protestants. They were the enemies of Mary of Lorraine and her Roman Catholic friends.

In a short time there were so many Protestants that the queen-mother had to let them worship in their own way. Knox could now return home.

HOW QUEEN MARY SAILED
FOR HER NATIVE LAND

John Knox reached Edinburgh on the 2nd May 1559. He had never been afraid of preaching in the days when it was unsafe to do so. Now he went through the length and breadth of the land trying to make all men Protestants.

None in Scotland could speak like him.

He could move men, and make them do as he pleased.

Many of the nobles became Protestants. They called themselves the " Lords of the Congregation." Their leader was Lord James Stewart, the queen's half-brother.

Mary of Lorraine began to repent of having yielded to the Protestants. She tried to take back her word, and war broke out. It was a civil war, for Scot fought against Scot.

The regent, as usual, got help from France. The Protestants were aided by the Queen of England. The Lords of the Congregation gained the day. The regent died, and it was arranged that the French troops should be sent home.

A parliament met in 1560. It decided that, from that time, Scotland was to be a Protestant country, and not a Roman Catholic one.

Meanwhile, in sunny France, Queen Mary and her four Maries led a gay and merry life. Everybody loved " the little Queen of Scots," and praised her sweet and gentle ways. The minstrels never tired of singing of her beauty.

When she was sixteen, she was married to Francis, the Dauphin or Prince of France. When his father died, he became king.

Mary now wore the crown both of Scotland and of France. She even said that she should have been Queen of England instead of her cousin, Queen Elizabeth.

Francis, Mary's husband, only lived for two years as king of France. Mary found she was not such a great lady in France when her husband was dead. So she made up her mind to return to her native land. She left for ever the fair land of France, where she had spent so many happy years.

The four Maries stood beside her as the shores of France became dim in the distance. When night fell, a bed was placed for her on deck. All night the ship lay becalmed. Early next morning, the wind blew fresh again. "Farewell," she murmured as the land of France faded away. " Farewell, beloved France, I shall never see thee more."

There was mist on land and sea when the two ships entered Leith harbour. The Scots did not expect her so soon, but the noise of cannon soon brought them forth to welcome their young and beautiful queen.

At night, bonfires blazed on every hill. Musicians played beneath her window. Some days after, the city looked its best as the queen rode from Holyrood to a great feast in the castle.

As in the days of James IV., the little girl-angels sang, the bells pealed a merry note, and the fountain at the Cross ran with wine.

On the very next Sunday, a great uproar was heard in those same streets. In France, the queen had been brought up as a Roman Catholic. But the new laws said that no one was " to say mass," as the Roman Catholic worship was called.

When Queen Mary ordered her Roman Catholic priest to preach in Holyrood Chapel, many rushed with drawn swords to kill him.

But Lord James Stewart defended him, and the service ended in peace. When Knox heard of it, he said, " One mass is more fearful to me than if ten thousand enemies landed in Scotland."

The queen, he thought, was only biding her time to bring the old religion back again.

THE STORY OF THE CHASEABOUT RAID

The gloomy Palace of Holyrood was a great change from the gay court of France. Yet Mary spent many happy days in her new home. In the early summer morning, she loved to walk in her gardens. There she had planted many trees. No queen of Scotland ever loved them as she did.

Then she would sit and sew with her faithful Maries. As they worked, her minstrels sang the songs of France that she loved so well.

Sometimes she would send for John Knox to come and speak with her. They would talk for hours about each other's religion. As John Knox was a Protestant, and Queen Mary a Roman Catholic, they could never agree. Once, as he spoke to her, she burst into tears.

From time to time her advisers came to the palace to help her to rule the land. Among them were her wise half-brother, and the cunning Maitland of Lethington.

They advised her to visit all parts of her realm. At the head of a gay company of lords and ladies, she set off on her first journey from castle to castle, from town to town. Wherever she went, she received gifts. The town of Perth gave her " a heart of gold full of gold."

Pleased with her welcome, she made a second journey farther north. On the road, the Earl of Huntly refused to open his gates to the queen.

The weather was cold, and food was dear. The corn lay late. Yet never was Queen Mary in better spirits.

" Ah," said she, " would that I knew what it was to be all night in the fields. Fain would I march with a steel-cap on my head, a Glasgow buckler at my back, and a broadsword at my side."

The clansmen of Huntly were soon put to flight. His lands were given to Lord James Stewart, who now became Earl of Moray.

So the first years of Mary's reign were happy. Many princes and nobles wished to marry her, but it was not easy for her to make up her mind. She even sent to Queen Elizabeth to ask her advice. " I shall marry anyone you choose, if you will say I am your heir," said Mary.

The two queens could never be friends. As long as she lived, Queen Elizabeth would never declare who was to wear the crown after her.

So Mary married her cousin, Lord Darnley. He was a very fine-looking man. He was also the next heir to the throne of England after Mary herself. This made Elizabeth fear her two cousins more than ever.

Darnley was also a Roman Catholic. Moray

now saw that Mary would never become a Protestant. His friends, the Lords of the Congregation, were also displeased. They took up arms.

The queen and her husband were ready for them. Many Scots gathered round their ruler. At their head rode Darnley, in gilded armour. At his side was Mary, with pistols at her saddle-bow.

They chased Moray and the other rebels across the Border. This was called the " Roundabout " or " Chaseabout Raid."

THE STORY OF RICCIO

The Chaseabout Raid showed that many of the people still loved and trusted the queen. This was the happiest time of her life in Scotland. After this, many sorrows came upon her.

She soon found out that her husband was nothing but a weak and foolish boy. He was called king because he was the queen's husband, but he wished to be really the ruler of the country.

He was also jealous of Riccio, the queen's Italian favourite. He was not handsome like Darnley, but no one sang so sweetly. Being her secretary, he wrote her letters. Wherever the queen was, there was Riccio.

Many of the Protestant lords hated him also. They thought that the Pope had sent him to help Mary to bring back the old religion.

So a plot was made to kill the favourite. One night, five hundred horsemen surrounded the Palace. A party entered the courtyard. Their leader was Lord Ruthven, who had been ill, and looked very pale.

He went to Darnley's room. From it a narrow winding stair led to the queen's chamber. Darnley alone had the key. He entered the presence of his wife as she was supping with some friends. Riccio was also there, helping to serve the queen.

Some minutes later, Ruthven, pale and haggard, came in with a drawn sword in his hand.

"What means this?" said the queen to Darnley. "I know not," was the false reply. "Let yon man Davie come forth," cried the stern Ruthven.

In vain Riccio clung to the queen's robes. In vain she strove to shield him. He was dragged from her chamber and stabbed to death.

Meanwhile, Darnley tried to comfort her by telling her that no harm was meant. But one of her maids brought word that all was over.

"Then," said Mary, drying her tears, "I will study revenge."

The Protestant lords now tried to govern the kingdom. Moray and his companions rode into Edinburgh the day after the murder. Two days later, they found that Darnley had fled to Dunbar with the queen. There the fugitives were welcomed by the Earl of Bothwell.

In a few days, Mary and her husband were back in Edinburgh, and the murderers had to escape to England. Afterwards she found it better to forgive some of them, but she could not pardon Darnley. No one trusted him, for he had betrayed both his wife and his friends.

In 1566 a son was born to the queen and Darnley. Great was the joy throughout the land. In Edinburgh alone, there were five hundred bonfires. A great service was held in the church of St Giles.

Yet Mary and Darnley were not any happier together. The queen had now another favourite, the Earl of Bothwell. He was a brave soldier, but a wicked man.

About this time Darnley fell ill at Glasgow, where his parents lived.

When the queen heard this, she went and visited him. Then they journeyed together to Edinburgh. Here Darnley was lodged in a house in the Kirk of Field, where Edinburgh University now stands.

The queen and her child were at Holyrood,

M

but every day she came to see her husband. The king and queen seemed to be friends again.

Meanwhile, by night, mysterious noises might have been heard in the house where Darnley lay. Bothwell's friends were filling the rooms beneath with gunpowder.

Bothwell had planned it all. On the last night he came himself, in secret, to see if all was ready.

In the dead of night, a noise like thunder was heard all over the city. The house had been blown up. The bodies of Darnley and his servant were found in the orchard close by.

"A QUEEN WITHOUT A CROWN"

It was Bothwell who first told the queen of the terrible deed. Soon all Scotland rang with the news. A great sum of money was promised to anyone who would point out the murderer.

No one dared to do so, but portraits of

Bothwell were stuck up all over Edinburgh. Underneath was written, " This is the murderer of the King."

All Mary's friends urged her to punish the guilty. " If you do not do this," said they, "your people will think that you are the guilty one."

This is the reason why Mary lost the love of the Scots. Bothwell was tried. He came to court, riding on Darnley's horse, with a company of four thousand men. The trial was a mockery. Of course he was declared " Not guilty."

Yet Mary trusted Bothwell more and more. One day she set off to Stirling Castle to see her child. On her way home to Edinburgh, she was surrounded by armed men. Bothwell, their captain, laid his hand on the bridle of the queen's horse. Then he led her away, like a captive, to his castle at Dunbar.

He put away his own wife. Within a few days, Bothwell and Mary were married. Mary was no happier. Two days after the marriage, she cried for a knife to stab herself.

Then the nobles decided to try to save Mary from Bothwell. As she and her husband were staying at Borthwick Castle, they were almost taken by surprise.

Bothwell fled, leaving his wife behind. Next day she joined him, having escaped by night, dressed like a page, booted and spurred.

Her husband gathered an army of desperate men. The nobles marched to meet them. The two armies faced each other at Carberry Hill, near Musselburgh.

Mary's troops had no heart for the fight. One by one her soldiers deserted, and her army melted away. Bothwell's courage failed also. Mary bade him save himself, and they parted, never to meet again.

Bothwell fled to Dunbar. Thence he escaped to sea. He became a pirate, and died in prison in a strange land.

When he was " two miles or more " off, Mary gave herself up to her nobles. They brought her to Edinburgh. No shouts of welcome cheered her as she was led to the provost's house, opposite the Market Cross. Nothing was heard but angry voices, crying out that she had murdered her husband, Darnley.

Afterwards she was taken to Loch Leven, in Kinross. In the castle on an island of this loch, she was kept a prisoner.

Hither one day came Lord Lindsay, and Lord Ruthven, the son of Riccio's murderer. They had been sent to make her sign three papers. In one, she gave up the crown to her infant son, Prince James. In the other two, she chose Moray as regent. Five days later, Prince James, thirteen months old, was crowned King of Scotland.

THE END OF QUEEN MARY

Slowly and sadly the days passed away, but Mary's courage never left her. Often her jailors had to be changed, because they all learned to pity her, and tried to save her.

There was one who was not sent away. He was but a page, Willie Douglas by name. He used to serve at the high table where the keeper of the prison supped.

Every night the keys of the castle were placed beside the keeper. One evening Willie Douglas dropped his napkin over them. As he lifted it, he lifted the keys also.

No time was lost. The queen and her maid were led out of the castle by the faithful page. He carefully locked every heavy gate behind them.

When the alarm was given, Mary and her friends could be seen in a little boat, waving to horsemen on the shore.

Nothing could be done, for the doors were locked. Douglas threw the keys into the loch. A hundred years ago they were found there.

Once more free, the queen hurried with her friends across the Forth. She stopped at Niddrie Castle, and then she rode to Hamilton. There she found her friends, the Hamiltons, at the head of six thousand men.

Meanwhile Moray gathered an army in the name of the king. The two armies met at Langside, now a part of Glasgow.

King's Men fought against Queen's Men. "There was the father against the son, and the brother against the brother."

Mary watched the battle from a hillock near Cathcart Castle. In fear and trembling she heard the shouts of "God and the King" growing louder and louder. Fainter and fainter grew those of her friends — "God and the Queen."

Her hopes were gone. She and Mary Livingston, with one or two others, galloped away southwards. The first day they rode sixty miles.

Then they came to Dumfries, and passed to Dundrennan Abbey. Here a council was held. What was to be done? Some said one thing, some another. Several advised her to go to France.

" I will go to England," said Mary at last. " Not there," pleaded her friends.

Mary would not listen. Her friends watched her as a little fishing-boat carried her over to the land of her enemy, Queen Elizabeth. They knew that all indeed was lost.

Mary had only escaped from one prison to be shut up in another. Her royal cousin never forgot that she claimed the crown of England.

For eighteen years the once gay Mary Stewart was carried from castle to castle. Many plots were made to free her. One was to kill Queen Elizabeth, and put Mary on the English throne. It was found out, and it was known that Mary had written to the plotters.

Forty judges were sent to Fotheringay Castle to try her. None came to plead her cause. She was found guilty, and condemned to death.

At first, Elizabeth could not think of putting her cousin to death, but at last she yielded. The messengers brought word to Mary.

" I fear not death," she said, " I am weary of being in this world." She spent the night before her execution in writing to her friends, bidding them farewell.

Next morning, the 7th February 1587, she was led forth to die. Her ladies wept, but she bade them dry their tears. " To-day," she said, " you see the end of Mary Stewart's miseries."

Calmly she placed her head on the block. Two strokes of the headsman's axe, and all was over. Thus died Mary Stewart, one of the most beautiful and most unhappy queens that ever lived.

WHY KING JAMES WENT TO
LONDON

On the night of the 24th March 1603, a horseman, covered with mud, might have been seen spurring his horse towards Edinburgh.

On, on he sped, till he drew rein at Holyrood Palace. He demanded to see the king. He was told that James was sleeping; but he said that he bore great news from England, and must see him.

So they wakened the king. The messenger, almost dead with fatigue, was brought to him. Kneeling down, he hailed James as King of Scotland, England, and Ireland.

Then he told the king his story. " As our good Queen Bess lay a-dying, a lady of the court told me that you had at last been chosen to succeed to the English throne.

" This lady promised to let me know whenever our queen was dead. At last I heard that the end was near. Ready for the road, I waited beneath the window of the chamber where the dying queen lay.

" Suddenly the window opened, and a ring was dropped to me. It was the signal. I knew that the queen was dead. That was but three nights ago. Long live your Majesty, James I., King of Scotland, England, and Ireland! "

Never had the journey from London been done so quickly. Right well the king praised the horseman, Sir Robert Carey, for his speed. He promised to reward him richly.

The news spread like wildfire. Next day the church of St Giles was crowded to see the king. Yes, there he was near the pulpit!

When the sermon was ended, he spoke to the people. " I am but going from one part of the isle to another. I had thought to need your armour. Now I need but your good wishes."

Two days later he set out for his new throne. It took him a month to reach London. Everywhere the English welcomed him heartily. The prison doors were opened, and many were set free.

When he entered London, perhaps he could not help thinking of some of his forefathers, and other brave Scots, who also had trod these same streets.

What of William the Lion and David II.? And what of Wallace, the hero of Scotland? What a difference now! And all this was happening because, one hundred years before, the Rose of England, Margaret, had married James IV.

Many Scots followed the king to England. Indeed, so many poor Scots left their native land, that James forbade any to do so who had not his special leave.

He did not like to hear the English saying:

> " ' Bonny Scot, all witness can,
> England has made thee a gentleman.' "

Some did indeed become rich. The king's jeweller, George Heriot, was one of them. He was so wealthy, that they called him " Jingling Geordie." When he died, he left his money to erect a school in Edinburgh for poor boys. You can see the fine building to this day.

James promised to come and see his people in the north every three years. But, though he lived till 1625, he only came once. During this visit he tried to make the Scots become Episcopalians, like most of his subjects in England.

Both countries were Protestant. In England, however, most of the people called themselves Episcopalians. They had bishops to rule over their ministers. There was music in the churches, and the ministers wore white gowns or surplices.

Now, the Scots were Presbyterians. They thought that the Episcopalian worship was too like the old religion they had given up. Besides, they did not want any new ways from England. So the changes that James ordered did not please the Scots. Many of the Scottish ministers would not do as the king commanded.

THE STORY OF JENNY GEDDES

It is a pity that Charles I., who became king in 1625, was not so wise as his father. He had been brought up in England, and he did not know very much about his people in the North.

He made up his mind to force the Scots to become Episcopalians. He visited Scotland in 1633, and everywhere he received a hearty welcome.

The crown of Scotland was placed on his head in Holyrood. Many of the Scottish people were angry when they found that Charles had brought his chief bishop, afterwards Archbishop Laud, with him.

So when Charles called together the Parliament of Scotland, he found that it was not very friendly towards him. Indeed, the king and Parliament almost quarrelled. It was about the old question of how to worship God.

When Charles reached London again, he sent back word that the English Prayer-Book was to be used in Scottish churches.

The Scots were not pleased at these changes, yet Charles paid no heed. In 1637 another Prayer-Book was sent to Scotland. The Scots thought that it had been written by Archbishop Laud, whom they so disliked.

They resolved not to use the book themselves, nor to let anyone else use it.

Now, on Sunday, the 23rd July 1637, the new book was to be read for the first time in the church of St. Giles, Edinburgh.

Great numbers came to church that day. There sat the chief nobles of Scotland, the judges, and other well-known people. In came the archbishop, the dean, and other ministers.

The preacher went up into the pulpit. He opened the book, and began to read.

Suddenly a stool came whizzing past his head. A woman's voice was heard crying, " False loon, dost thou say mass at my lug? "

The folding-stool had been thrown by Jenny Geddes, a woman who kept a cabbage stall in the High Street. In those days, each one brought his own seat to church.

At once there was the greatest uproar. People rushed up the pulpit steps and tore the surplice from the preacher's shoulders. The Archbishop then tried to speak. " Pull him down! stone him! " was the cry.

Outside the church the crowd was great, and the Archbishop and his friends barely escaped with their lives.

All over the country, people would not hear the new book read. Yet Charles was stubborn, and would not give in.

So, on the 28th February 1638, a great event took place in Greyfriars Church, in Edinburgh.

It was crowded with people, eager to sign a great sheet of paper. This paper said that all who wrote their names on it, promised to defend the worship of their forefathers against the king.

Many wished to add their names. Some think that the " Covenant," as the paper was called, was carried outside into the churchyard, and that there " a flat gravestone served as a desk."

Everybody signed it—nobles, gentry, wealthy burghers, tradesmen, and shopkeepers. Copies of the Covenant were sent all over the land, and everywhere it was signed.

In November, King Charles had to yield. The new Prayer-Book, the bishops, and the surplices were all done away with.

HOW THE SCOTS FOUGHT IN
ENGLAND

The Covenanters, as those who signed the Covenant were called, soon learned that Charles was only biding his time. He never intended to keep his promise.

Word came to Scotland that Charles was gathering an army to force the Scots to become

Episcopalians. The Covenanters, therefore, took up arms.

Their leader was Alexander Leslie, a brave soldier who had fought many battles in foreign lands. The Earl of Argyle, and the Earl of Montrose, were also good and trusty men. Montrose loved the sound of battle, wherever glory was to be won.

Then an army marched to the Borders against the king. The Covenanters pitched their tents on Dunse Law, in Berwickshire.

Twelve miles away lay the royal army, but the king's men were not eager for battle. Many of the soldiers were friendly to the Scots.

So King Charles again agreed to give up trying to have bishops, and surplices, and prayer-books, in Scottish churches.

Once more he did not keep his word, and once again the Covenanting army marched south. This time they crossed the Tweed.

The king saw that the Scots were in earnest. He afterwards went to Edinburgh, and gave the Scots everything they wanted.

Indeed, he was too friendly. The Covenanters began to think there must be some reason for the king's kindness. They were quite right. The king had quarrelled with his Parliament in England. He had insisted on doing as he liked, without asking the advice of Parliament.

War soon broke out in that country. It was
a civil war. Englishmen fought against Englishmen. On the one side were the Parliament and
most of the townsfolk; on the other, the king,
the nobles, and many of the country-people.

The Scots were never sure that Charles would
keep his promise. So they took the side of the
Parliament, and fought against the king. Many
on that side were Presbyterians, like the Scots.

While the Scottish army was in England it
was sorely needed at home. Montrose declared
that he would never draw his sword against the
king. So with two friends he slipped back into
Scotland.

He made his way in secret to the Forest of
Athole, where the Highlanders had come
together. What a welcome the wild clansmen
gave him! The sky was dark with the bonnets
in the air.

Many Irish had also come over to help King
Charles. They had but few arms. "There are
plenty of stones," said Montrose. "Use them
first. You will soon have guns and swords."

These were brave men, and would follow
Montrose to death. They were, however, very
cruel. They would kill a man with as little pity
as they would kill a beast.

HOW THE GREAT MARQUIS
FOUGHT AND DIED IN SCOTLAND

It was with soldiers like these that the " Great Marquis"—for Charles made Montrose a marquis —fought and won for the king. We cannot tell all his adventures, and how he gained his battles.

In one year he put the Covenanters six times to flight. His great enemy was the Earl of Argyle, who had also been made a marquis. After Montrose's third victory, the earl set off to chase him from the Highlands. But Montrose only fought when he liked.

> " He who fights and runs away,
>   May live to fight another day."

That was what he must have said to himself.

Argyle, tired of chasing his enemy, shut himself up in his strong castle of Inverlochy, at the foot of Ben Nevis, on the shores of Loch Eil. There he meant to spend the winter.

The weather was cold. Snow covered the mountains, and made great drifts amid the hills. Yet, late one night, Argyle heard that Montrose was near. The marquis had led his troops across swollen torrents, through desolate glens, over steep mountains.

At daybreak, Argyle was rowed in a boat to the middle of the loch. There, in safety, he watched his clansmen fight. The army of

N

Montrose had marched twenty miles the day before. Yet the Highlanders were eager for the battle as their trumpeters blew a blast for the king.

The clansmen of Montrose first fired their pistols. Then drawing their claymores, they rushed down upon the enemy. Argyle's men were completely routed.

After gaining other three battles in the North, Montrose marched to the Borders to win the South of Scotland for the king.

By this time, part of the Covenanting army had crossed the Cheviots, to try to conquer the king's general. They heard that Montrose's army lay at Philiphaugh, a meadow by the river Ettrick, near Selkirk.

Marching quickly, they overtook the enemy. Most of Montrose's Highlanders had long since gone home to their glens, laden with booty. His soldiers that were left were not so brave, and they were soon defeated by the Covenanters. Montrose had to flee to France.

The king had lost both in England and in Scotland. In 1649 he was beheaded. The soldiers of the English Parliament would not have another king, and the Parliament governed the country.

The Scots offered the crown of Scotland to Charles, the son of Charles I., if he would sign

the Covenant. Charles was very unwilling to
do so. He thought he might try to win back
his father's crown himself. So he sent Montrose
back to Scotland, to raise
the royal flag again in the
Highland glens.

Montrose, a prisoner, passing
Moray House, Edinburgh, the
house of Argyle. He had come
to Edinburgh disguised as a
beggar.

This time the Covenanters were ready for him. He could not gather a great army, and he was taken prisoner.

At Edinburgh, he was ordered to be hanged like a traitor. He was placed in a cart, and driven from the Water Gate, near Holyrood, to the Tolbooth Prison.

When he was led forth to die, he was dressed as if he were going to a wedding. His flowing hair fell over a scarlet cloak covered with lace. So noble did he look, that many wept.

Thus died Montrose, on the 21st May 1650.

A KINGDOM WITHOUT A KING

When Charles knew that the "Great Marquis" was executed, he agreed to sign the Covenant. He would have signed a hundred covenants, if only he might thereby be king.

When he came to Edinburgh, he was welcomed right royally. Yet he soon grew tired of the Covenanters and their long sermons. He would have liked to get rid of them, but he knew he could never come to his own again without their help.

Now, while Charles was living gloomily among his new friends, Oliver Cromwell, who had been appointed Lord Protector of England,

was gathering an army.   He was going to punish
the Scots for welcoming Charles.

Cromwell set out for Scotland, like Edward I.
in the olden days.   While he marched along
the coast, a fleet by sea carried the food for
the army.

The Scots also did as their forefathers had
done.   When Cromwell came to the Borders, he
found that his enemies had scarcely left a blade
of grass for his horses.

Keeping close to his fleet, he came near
Edinburgh.   There General David Leslie was
waiting for him.   So Cromwell and his brave
troops had to retreat.   It must have been with
heavy hearts, for the " Ironsides," as these
soldiers were called, had never known before
what it was to retreat.

The skilful Leslie followed close behind.
The very day that Cromwell entered Dunbar,
the Scottish general encamped on a hill above
the town.

Never had Cromwell been in such danger.
He could get no food for his army.   The soldiers
began to die of want and disease.

Cromwell looked anxiously at the hill above
him, where the Scottish banners fluttered in the
breeze.   One morning, he could scarcely believe
his eyes.   There were the Scots moving down
the hills to meet him on the plain!

It was too true. "The Lord hath delivered them into our hands," the Lord Protector is said to have exclaimed. His Ironsides simply drove the Scots before them. Cromwell only lost twenty men. Of the Scots, four thousand were killed, and ten thousand taken prisoner. This battle, called "Dunbar Drove," took place on the 3rd September 1650.

Then Charles gathered another army, which he led into England. But Cromwell overtook him at Worcester, on the 3rd September 1651, exactly one year after the battle and completely routed the Scots of Dunbar, again.

After many adventures, Charles escaped from England. Soon Scotland lay at Cromwell's feet. As in the days of Edward I., English soldiers were placed in every town and castle.

The only stronghold that held out for Charles was Dunnottar Castle, in Kincardine-shire.

It was a very strong castle, and into it the Scots had carried the royal crown, the sceptre, and the sword of state.

This made Cromwell's officers all the more eager to capture it. They besieged it closely, and soon the gallant defenders had little food left.

They knew that they would soon have to

Hiding the " Honours " of Scotland

yield, so they made a great effort to save the crown.

A brave minister and his wife hit upon a plan. This lady, Mrs Grainger, asked leave to enter the castle.

The English were very polite, and said she might do so. She entered the castle, and was allowed to carry away some bundles of lint. Nobody suspected, as she rode calmly through their camp, that the " Honours " as they are called, were snugly hidden underneath her bundles.

The little garrison then gave themselves up. Although they were cruelly treated, not one would tell where the crown lay hidden.

It had been buried beneath the minister's pulpit. Afterwards, when the king came to his own again, the brave lady and her husband were rewarded for their loyal deed.

HOW THE KING CAME HOME AGAIN

On the 26th May 1660, the streets of Edinburgh were gay with people on holiday. The town was decorated. A fountain at the town cross ran wine. Nothing was heard but the clinking and the smashing of glasses, for in those days, when a great person's health was drunk, the wineglass was broken at once.

At night, bonfires were kindled in every street and on every hill. Even Jenny Geddes, it is said, brought baskets and shelves from her cabbage-stall to help the blaze.

Why all this joy? It is that the king has come to his own again. Charles II. now reigned over England, Scotland, and Ireland.

For eight years after the taking of Dunnottar Castle, Cromwell's generals ruled the land. They governed Scotland well. Even the fierce Highlanders had to obey the laws.

In 1658 Cromwell died, on the 3rd of September, the day of Dunbar and Worcester. After his death, his son became Lord Protector, but he was not a soldier like his father. He soon went back to his farm, to live quietly and peacefully.

Then Cromwell's soldiers tried to rule the land, but the people got tired of them. They were always quarrelling among themselves.

At last a Parliament was held. It decided to welcome Charles home again. Everywhere there was great rejoicing as at Edinburgh.

The Scots remembered that Charles had signed the Covenant. They thought they would be allowed to worship in their own way.

The Covenanters sent Sharp, one of their ministers, to London, to remind the king of his signing the Covenant. But Sharp came home to be made Archbishop of St Andrews.

Then bishops were again placed over the churches, as in the days of Charles I. All the ministers who would not obey them were put out of their churches.

Between two and three hundred refused to obey the new law. Other ministers were put in their places. These were mostly ignorant men, some even ploughmen, and the people would not go to hear them preach.

They used to gather in barns and farmhouses to listen to the voice of their own minister. The churches were empty.

A new law was therefore passed. All who would not go to church were to be made to pay large sums of money.

Then the congregations began to meet in secret among the hills, besides a morass, perhaps, or a river-bed. Watchers on the hilltop kept a look-out for the king's soldiers, who were in search of them.

THE STORY OF THE COVENANTERS

The " Conventicles," as these meetings among the hills were called, were often found out, and the Covenanters taken by surprise. Then the prisoners were led before judges, and they had to pay large sums of money before they were set free.

At last some of the Covenanters took up arms. They marched towards Edinburgh, hoping that many would join them.

But when the king's troops came upon them at Rullion Green, amid the Pentland Hills, their numbers were fewer than before. The Covenanters were completely defeated, and many were captured.

Some were hanged, and others were cruelly tortured with the " boot." This was a kind of wooden framework placed over the leg; then wedges were driven in between the limb and the boot so as to cause great pain.

Later, " thumbscrews " were used for the same wicked purpose. A thumbscrew was a sort of ring which was slipped over the thumb. Then the ring was screwed tight till the finger was crushed.

Yet the Covenanters would not give up what they believed to be true. Another way to punish them was chosen. Six thousand wild

Highlanders were sent into Ayrshire, to plunder those who would not obey the new laws.

In 1679 Archbishop Sharp was murdered by twelve Covenanters. They dragged him out of his carriage, and slew him before his daughter's eyes. He had once been a Covenanter. When he afterwards became an Episcopalian, he cruelly treated his former friends.

The struggle grew fiercer. That same year the Covenanters again gathered an army. In June they defeated the king's troops, under Graham of Claverhouse, at Loudon Hill, in Ayrshire. But in the same month they were put to flight by the Duke of Monmouth, at Bothwell Bridge.

A strange prison was chosen for those taken after the battle. For five months a thousand Covenanters lived as prisoners in Greyfriars Churchyard, in Edinburgh. Perhaps some of them had signed the Covenant in that place forty years before.

There they lay in all kinds of weather. Only when winter came, were a few huts put up to shelter them.

At length some were set free, but many died. The rest were put on board ship, and sent away to America, to work as slaves under a broiling sun. The vessel was lost, and nearly all were drowned.

When Charles II. died in 1695, his brother, James VII., became king. He was a Roman Catholic. The " Killing Time," as it was called, now began.

Graham of Claverhouse spent most of his time man-hunting. With his soldiers at his back, he chased the Covenanters across the desolate moors, and hunted them out of their hiding-places. When they were caught, some were shot on the spot, and others had one ear cut off, and were shipped to America to be sold as slaves.

All this time, James VII. really wished to make his people, both in England and Scotland, Roman Catholics like himself. He sent away his Protestant advisers, and chose those of his own religion. All the officers in the army had also to be Roman Catholics.

When the chief men in England saw this, they sent to Holland, and asked William of Orange to come over and be their king. He was a Protestant, and had married James's daughter, Mary.

When he crossed to England in 1688, James had to flee to France; for all his friends, even his daughter, had left him.

So William, and Mary his wife, became the sovereigns of England, Scotland, and Ireland.

" BONNIE DUNDEE "

On the day that William and Mary were crowned in Westminster Abbey, a great crowd gathered round the Market Cross in Edinburgh.

The townsfolk had come to hear William and Mary proclaimed the sovereigns of Scotland, England, and Ireland. Round the Market Cross stood the heralds, dressed in velvet coats, with the flags of the three nations sewn on them.

Each held in his hand a long roll of paper. Each unrolled it, and began to read the new law, one after the other.

When they had finished, the trumpeters blew a blast, and William and Mary were King and Queen of Scotland. The Scots had chosen the same king and queen as England, because they were both Protestants.

James, however, had many friends in Scotland. The Episcopalians were almost all on his side. The Highlanders also wished James to be king instead of William, and they were always ready to fight when they had a leader. They did find a leader—Graham of Claverhouse, of whom you have read. He was now called Viscount Dundee.

When Dundee raised the king's flag on the hills of the North, three thousand clansmen gathered to fight. The king's troops, under General Mackay, marched north to give battle to the Highlanders.

Bonnie Dundee

As they drew near Blair Atholl, where Dundee was encamped, they had to go through the deep Pass of Killiecrankie. Slowly they made their way. Scarce two could march abreast, and the river Garry roared beneath.

When they had all marched through this rocky pass, they saw the clansmen drawn up for battle.

Mackay placed his men in line three deep across the mouth of the pass. After watching the king's army for two weary hours, the Highlanders rushed against the enemy to the sound of the bagpipes.

They stopped a moment to fire their pistols. Then throwing them away, and drawing their claymores, they rushed on the thin line, yelling their war-cries.

The king's troops had never had to fight in this way before. " In two minutes the battle was lost and won." Mackay's men were driven down the pass.

Shortly after the fight began, Dundee, riding in front of his men, fell from his horse, struck by a musket ball.

" How goes the day? " he asked. " Well for King James," answered a soldier. " If it is well for him, it matters less for me," said the dying Graham.

On the death of Dundee, the Highlanders went back to their native glens. " The war," as King William said, " ended with Dundee's life."

"THE VALE OF TEARS"

Although the war ended so quickly, many of the Highlanders were still unwilling to obey King William and Queen Mary.

So the chiefs were compelled to take an oath that they would obey William and Mary. If they did not take the oath by the 1st January 1692, they were to be put to death.

One by one the chiefs yielded. But one of them—MacIan, the head of the Macdonalds of Glencoe—was stubborn, and held out to the last. He lived in a wild valley formed by the river Coe, which falls into Loch Leven, in Argyleshire. His clan was one of the wildest in the Highlands.

At last MacIan learnt that all the chiefs had given in except himself. Then he set off in haste to Fort William to take the oath before the governor of this castle.

There he learned that he had gone to the wrong person. He had to walk to Inveraray, where lived the king's judge.

It was in the depths of winter. The white-haired old man could not travel swiftly across the snow-covered mountains, and the deep torrents, as in the days gone by.

When he came to Inveraray, he was three

o

days late. However, the judge was a kindly man, and later MacIan took the oath. When he reached home he was pleased to think that all was well.

One morning, word came that a number of king's troops were marching up the lonely glen. They were Campbells, the Macdonalds' most bitter foes.

Filled with alarm, MacIan's sons went to meet them. " Come ye as friends or foes? " they shouted. " As friends," came the reply.

They received a right good welcome. For a fortnight the soldiers lived on the best of fare. The days were spent in hunting. At night they played at games by the hearthside of their new friends.

What had brought the king's soldiers to Glencoe? It had been told to the king that MacIan had not taken the oath at the appointed time. The king thought, therefore, that the Macdonalds should be punished.

So William had signed an order to root out " the den of thieves," according to the law. That was why the soldiers had come to the glen.

At last, on the 12th February, the captain of the king's troops was ordered to fall upon those who had treated him so kindly.

That night the deed was done. Shots rang out in the stillness of the night. They murdered the old chief by his own hearth stone. No mercy was shown, even to women and children. The houses were burned. Some escaped, half-naked, to the hills, but many of these died amid the snow, or perished of hunger.

All Scotland rang with the terrible crime. Men could scarce believe that a king could have given such an order.

It was too true; though William had not thought that the law would be carried out in such a terrible way. The Scots never forgave the king for his carelessness.

HOW TWO PARLIAMENTS WERE JOINED

Although the Crowns of England and Scotland had been united in 1603, the Scots and the English had never been very friendly.

The Massacre of Glencoe made many people in Scotland think that it would be better to have a king of their own. Another thing happened which made many Scotsmen still more angry with William.

About this time the Scots made a plan to trade across the seas with America. Many left their native land, to build a new city at Darien, between North and South America.

When they arrived there, they had to fight the Spaniards, who had been there before them. Numbers died in battle, others of want and disease.

In many homes in Scotland there was sadness, on account of the friends and the money that had been lost. Every one believed that William might have helped his people in the North more than he did.

So there was much discontent in Scotland. King William thought that the best plan would be to join the two Parliaments. Then the Scots would send chosen men to sit in Parliament, in London, to help him to rule the two countries.

William died before he could carry this out. The next to wear the crown was Anne, the daughter of James VII.

The English Parliament made a law which said that, if all the queen's children died, the crown was to go to Sophia, grand-daughter of James VI., and her heirs. She had married a Prince of Germany.

But the Scots were still so angry with the English, that the Parliament of Scotland made another law. It said that the ruler of Scotland after Queen Anne might not be the same person as reigned in England.

The Scots were especially angry because the English would not allow them to trade with their colonies.

The English began to get alarmed. They fortified some towns on the Borders. The Scots began to drill, as if they were preparing to fight.

It would have been a great pity if the two countries had gone to war. So, in 1706, men were sent from Scotland to London to try to bring about a union of the two Parliaments.

Many Scots would not hear of such a plan. Many would have liked to bring James VII. or his heirs back to the throne again. There would be little hope of doing so, if the two Parliaments became one.

The Presbyterians were afraid that the Episcopalians in England would try to make Scotland Episcopalian. The nobles thought they would not be such great persons in a great united Parliament.

The Scottish Parliament met to talk the matter over. The citizens of Edinburgh crowded the High Street. They cheered all the members who did not wish for union. All the others were hissed.

There was great quarrelling in the Parliament; but at last, in 1707, it was decided that there should be one Parliament for England and Scotland.

Scotland was to send forty-five members to sit in the House of Commons in London, and sixteen lords in the House of Lords.

Scotland was to have her own ancient laws, her own judges, and her own Presbyterian worship. The two countries were to be called Great Britain.

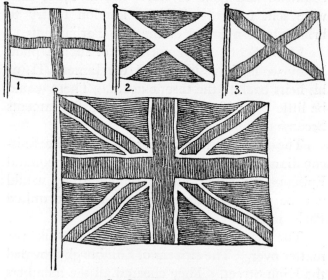

1. St. George of England.
2. St. Andrew of Scotland.
3. St. Patrick of Ireland.

A new flag was made, by placing the red cross of St George of England on the white cross of St Andrew of Scotland.

About one hundred years later, in 1800, the cross of St Patrick of Ireland was put on the top of these two.

That flag is called the "Union Jack." Jack is like the French word for James, the first king to unite the crowns of the two countries.

It was long before Scotland liked the Union of the Parliaments. They spoke of the members who voted for it as "those who had sold their country."

Nowadays, we see that it was a good thing for Scotland. The two nations became more friendly. Trade increased; both the towns and the country became prosperous. Scotland became a rich land, and its great men helped to rule Great Britain and Ireland.

A HUNTING PARTY, AND WHAT CAME OF IT

When Queen Anne died, George I., the son of Sophia, grand-daughter of James VI., became king.

Now, though James VII. had died in France, a son of his was living in that country. He was called "James the Pretender," because he claimed to be the true king of Great Britain and Ireland.

Many people both in Scotland and in England thought that he should have been king. They were called " Jacobites," which means " followers of James."

George I. was a German, and could not speak English. The Jacobites laughed at such a king. They called him the " Wee German Lairdie." They longed for the time when the " king over the water " would come home again.

So the Pretender thought that he had now a good chance of winning back the crown his fathers had worn.

He sent the Earl of Mar to Scotland. When this nobleman reached his estates in Braemar, in Aberdeenshire, he invited the chiefs to a great hunting party.

They all came, accompanied by many of their clansmen, to help to drive the deer. So the days seemed to pass in hunting and feasting.

Yet, every day, meetings were held in secret, and at last it was agreed to take up arms for " James VIII. of Scotland."

On the 6th September 1715, the chiefs unfurled their banner. The day was stormy, and the gilt ball on the top of the flag-pole fell off. The Highlanders thought this was unlucky.

However, they scattered to their castles and

glens to raise more clansmen to fight for a Stewart king.

In those days there was no penny post, and no telegraphs, or railways. How, then, did the Highland warriors in lonely glens know when to gather for war?

When a chief wanted to assemble his clansmen, he took two branches of wood, and made them into a rough kind of cross.

The ends were burnt in the fire, and then dipped in goat's blood. Then picking out the swiftest runner of his clan, he bade him carry this signal. Away he rushed, telling all he met his lord's commands. When he reached the end of his journey, he entered the first house he came to, and gave the " Fiery Cross," as it was called, to the eldest son.

This man carried it to the next village. In a very short time, all the clansmen were marching to the meeting-place.

In this way Mar gathered his army. The Duke of Argyle was the general of King George's troops.

The two armies came in sight of each other at Sheriffmuir, in the south of Perthshire. Each army was posted on a high hill, with a lower rising ground between them.

That night, Mar gathered the chiefs together. " Fight or not fight? " he asked. " Fight," they cried with one voice, tossing their bonnets in the air.

Their shouts reached the ears of the clansmen, who replied by yelling their war-cries.

When the fight began, the two armies rushed to try to seize the hill between them. Before they were aware, they met on the hilltop.

Instead of attacking King George's troops before they got over their surprise, Mar let the precious moments pass away. "Oh, for one hour of Dundee," cried an old chief, as Mar still waited.

Then a very curious thing happened. The right of Argyle's army defeated the left of Mar's, and the right half of Mar's put the left of Argyle's to flight.

No one can tell who won this battle; but at nightfall, Mar retreated from the battlefield. A month later, a thin, pale-looking, young man joined him. It was "James VIII." His look was sad, and his speech was slow.

Almost immediately he began to talk of going back. This was not the kind of king for clansmen.

"If he is willing to die like a prince," they said, "he shall see there are ten thousand men in Scotland willing to die with him."

But the Pretender was not a hero. Shortly after, he and Mar left the army secretly, and set sail for France. The Highlanders scattered among their mountains and glens. The " Fifteen," as it was called from the year 1715, had come to an end.

" BONNIE PRINCE CHARLIE "

Thirty years passed away, and still the Pretender did not come again to claim his own. He was now too old to lead men to battle.

But he had a son, Charles Edward Stewart, who was ready to risk all to win a crown. He was called the " Young Pretender," or the " Young Chevalier." But in their songs the Jacobites sang of him as " Bonnie Prince Charlie."

In 1745, word came that his ship lay off the west coast of Scotland. He sent for the neighbouring chiefs to come on board. They had always hoped that, when their prince came, he would have French troops at his back.

When they saw that he had come alone, they advised him to go back to France. But a young man, standing by, grasped his sword, as if angry at what the chiefs had said.

" You at least will join me," said the prince.

" I will follow you to death, though all should leave you," said the brave clansmen.

So the others agreed to fight under the Young Chevalier's banner. The prince now came ashore at Moidart, in Inverness-shire. He had brought but seven men with him to try to gain a throne. These were known as the " Seven men of Moidart."

On the 25th July 1745, the prince's flag was raised at Glenfinnan. This time no gilt ball fell as the red and white silk banner was unfurled.

It was held by the Marquis of Tullibardine. So old was this chief, that two men had to help him to raise it.

Here now gathered the Camerons, the clan of the " Gentle Lochiel," the Stewarts of Appin, the Macdonalds of Glencoe, and many another Highland clan.

When news of this reached London the advisers of George II., who was then king, were greatly alarmed. They had but few soldiers to fight the Young Pretender, for most of the regular troops were in a distant land, fighting the French.

However, the king's general, Sir John Cope, gathered as many men as he could, and set out to meet the prince. But, as he marched through the Highlands, his soldiers began to desert. Many were Highlanders, and wished to fight for the Stewarts.

The army of the Young Chevalier was in high spirits. They loved their prince. Did he not

Raising the Standard
at Glenfinnan
July 1745

walk at their head with a targe on his back,
joking with his men? On the day that he put
on a pair of brogues, or Highland shoes, he said,
" Before I throw these off, I shall fight General
Cope."

But Cope lost heart as his army melted away.
He turned off towards Inverness, leaving the road
to Edinburgh open to the prince.

Charles pushed on to the capital. As his
army drew near, the burghers were in great
fear.

They had heard dreadful stories about the
Highlanders, and thought that they would slay
every man in the city.

So the townsfolk armed themselves for battle.
One day they set out from the Grassmarket to
fight for their city. At the last moment, many
went back to say a last farewell to those at home.
They all forgot to come back. Only one was
brave enough to march outside the city wall!

Lochiel with his men lay in wait near the city
gates, hoping to get inside.

Just as he was about to return to camp, the
gates were opened to let a carriage enter.
Lochiel and his clansmen rushed in behind the
carriage, and Edinburgh was taken for Prince
Charles.

Next day the Young Chevalier rode into the
city at the head of his army. A gallant young

man he looked, as he rode on his white horse. He wore a short tartan coat, and the kilt. On his head was a blue bonnet, decorated with the white rose of the Jacobites. Many thought he was like Robert the Bruce.

That night, he slept in Holyrood Palace, the home of his forefathers.

THE BATTLE OF PRESTONPANS

In the meantime, Sir John Cope had made up his mind to fight. He sailed from Aberdeen, and arrived at Dunbar. Then he set out to march towards Edinburgh.

Next day, Prince Charles led his army to battle. They passed over the fields where, in days of old, Pinkie Cleugh had been fought.

Very early next day, before the sun rose, Charles led his army to the fight. As he stood before the Highlanders, he waved his sword in the air. " Gentlemen," he cried, " I have thrown away my scabbard." He meant to conquer or to die.

In the grey of the morning, the Highlanders came suddenly upon the army of King George. For a moment, they raised their bonnets as they said a short prayer. Then they fired their muskets. Drawing their claymores, they rushed furiously on the king's troops.

In a few minutes all was over. Sir John Cope fled as fast as his horse could carry him to Dunbar. Everyone laughed at a general who was the first to bring news of his own defeat.

Charles stayed in Holyrood for six weeks. It would have been much better if he had marched at once into England. Most of the king's troops had not yet come home, and the people of London were in great fear.

At the end of six weeks, Prince Charles said farewell to all his Edinburgh friends, and set off for London. On the march, he walked at the head of his men, talking cheerily, and in the best of spirits.

But after they had crossed the Border, few Jacobites joined his banner. The Highlanders felt far from home, and would fain have been back among their native hills again.

They reached Derby, near the centre of England. Here the chiefs came to Prince Charles, and told him that their clansmen would go no farther. In vain the Chevalier pleaded with them. " Rather than go back," he said, " I wish I were twenty feet underground." Not another step would they go.

With heavy hearts, the clansmen turned their faces homewards. Their leader no longer led them as before, but kept gloomily in the rear.

By this time, the king's troops were back

in England again, and three armies, one under the Duke of Cumberland, were in hot pursuit.

At Falkirk, Charles won a victory over General Hawley. Yet his men still continued to scatter to their homes. Food became scarce, and Prince Charles had still to retreat, with Cumberland at his heels.

THE LAST BATTLE

At Culloden Moor, near Inverness, the Duke of Cumberland met the army of Prince Charles.

At first the Highlanders tried to surprise the king's troops. They marched by night to within three miles of the enemy's camp, but by this time it was daylight, and they had to retreat. Weary and hungry, they fell back upon Culloden.

Before they had rested themselves, the duke and his men were upon them. Tired as they were, they had to get ready for battle.

As usual, they made a furious rush on the duke's army. But the king's troops now knew how to fight the Highlanders.

They were drawn up in two lines. When the first line had given way, Prince Charlie's men found another, with loaded muskets, ready for them.

In three quarters of an hour the fight was

over. On the left, the Macdonalds were shot down with great slaughter. They had refused to fight, because they were not placed on the right, the place of honour.

Prince Charles tried to gather his men again for the fight, but in vain. At the last moment, an officer laid hold of his horse's bridle, and led him from the field. The " Forty-five," as it was called from the year 1745, was over.

The Duke of Cumberland treated the clansmen very cruelly. Hundreds were shot down as they fled. Even the wounded were killed next day as they lay on the field of battle. All the houses round about were searched.

Meanwhile, Prince Charlie fled to the mountains. Though the poor Highlanders knew that thirty thousand pounds would be given for his head, none would betray him.

Yet he had to flee from one hiding-place to the other. Sometimes he wandered for days without food. At last he crossed over to South Uist, in the Hebrides.

There he lived in a forester's hut, while all around the king's soldiers and sailors were looking for him. At length they heard of his whereabouts. They surrounded the island, so that there was no chance of escape.

It was then that Flora Macdonald made up her mind to save Bonnie Prince Charlie. She

dressed him as her servant, calling him " Betty
Burke." As they journeyed along the road,
Betty got many a scolding for not doing her
work well!

At other times people would wonder why
Flora kept such a queer-looking maid. " Look,"
said a little girl once, " what long steps that
servant takes! "

Travelling in this way, they reached Skye.
After many other adventures, Bonnie Prince
Charlie escaped to France. The Jacobites
hoped he would come " over the water," and
win back his own again. They often sang that

> " Many a heart would break in twa,
>   Should he ne'er come back again."

But the prince never came again; and he died a
stranger in a far country.

" SCOTLAND FOR EVER! "

Many changes took place in Scotland after
the " Forty-five." The Highland chiefs were
not allowed to rule their clansmen any more.
They were governed by the king, like other
Scots.

At length a clever adviser of George III.
said, " Why not make these brave men soldiers
of the king? " So the chiefs gathered many of
their clansmen again. But this time it was to

fight for their countrymen, and not against them.

On many a field of battle, the old Highland war-cries were heard again. At Waterloo, the charge of the Scots Greys took place, and the Highland regiment—the Gordon Highlanders—rushed forward shouting, " Scotland for Ever! " In fighting for their country, they had learned a new war-cry.

It was not only by fighting that Scotsmen—Highlanders and Lowlanders—won fame. Some like James Watt, toiled in the workshop. When he was a boy, his aunt, with whom he lived, used to scold him for his idleness. He would sit watching the steam raising the lid of the kettle. He seemed to be idle, but he was thinking all the time. " If steam can raise a kettle-lid, perhaps I could make it move a wheel," said he to himself. That was how James Watt came to make the first steam-engine.

Others, like Robert Burns, sang of the country that gave them birth, or, like Sir Walter Scott, told its story. Many sailed to strange lands, so that they became " Britons beyond the Seas."

But whatever they did, and wherever they went, they were always proud that they were Scots. They tried to be faithful and true, like their forefathers in days of old.